FARM
DIY

Farm DIY

CompanionHouse Books™ is an imprint of Fox Chapel Publishers International Ltd.

Project Team
Vice President—Content: Christopher Reggio
Acquisition Editor: Bud Sperry
Editor: Jeremy Hauck
Copy Editor: Laura Taylor
Design: David Fisk
Index: Jay Kreider

ISBN 978-1-62008-332-1

The Cataloging-in-Publication Data is on file with the Library of Congress.

This book has been published with the intent to provide accurate and authoritative information in regard to the subject matter within. While every precaution has been taken in the preparation of this book, the author and publisher expressly disclaim any responsibility for any errors, omissions, or adverse effects arising from the use or application of the information contained herein. The techniques and suggestions are used at the reader's discretion and are not to be considered a substitute for veterinary care. If you suspect a medical problem, consult your veterinarian.

Fox Chapel Publishing   Fox Chapel Publishers International Ltd.
903 Square Street   7 Danefield Road, Selsey (Chichester)
Mount Joy, PA 17552   West Sussex PO20 9DA, U.K.

www.facebook.com/companionhousebooks

We are always looking for talented authors. To submit an idea, please send a brief inquiry to acquisitions@foxchapelpublishing.com.

Printed and bound in China
22 21 20 19   2 4 6 8 10 9 7 5 3 1

FARM
DIY

& Daniel Johnson
& Samantha Johnson

20 Useful and Fun Projects
for Your Farm or Homestead

COMPANION HOUSE
B O O K S

CONTENTS

20

Build a Bee House

30

Make a Candy Board for Honey Bees

38

Extract and Bottle Honey

46

Build a Goat Seesaw

54

Build a Log Jack

62

Paint a Barn

68

Plant a Fruit Tree

78

Protect a Fruit Tree

86

Build a Rabbit Nest Box

92

Build Sawhorses

98

Build a Stone Boat

106

Build a Stone Crib

112

Build a Beehive

124

Build a Goat Stand

134

Build a Farmers' Market Display Stand

142

Build a Rabbit Tractor

154

Make Cottage Cheese

160

Build a Barn Quilt

172

Graft a Fruit Tree

178

Build a Barn/Stable Medicine Cabinet

INTRODUCTION

Hello, DIYers! We're glad you're here to join us on what we hope is a fun and productive journey through twenty do-it-yourself farm projects.

Farmers through the centuries have proven themselves to be nothing if not self-reliant. The true farmer—whether farming as a full-time occupation, or simply as a hobby to add some self-sufficiency to life—is a jack-of-all-trades. Farmers rely on themselves to hammer, screw, saw, dig, weld, and paint their way through farm life, happily and effectively repairing, improvising, and building the items and infrastructure they need to get the job done.

And that's where this book comes in. We'll introduce you to twenty farm projects, outline the concepts involved, and demonstrate at least one potential method for getting the job done. In some cases, you might want to follow our ideas exactly, using the measurements, tools, and steps as we outline them. Other times, you might want to improvise on the basic concept—as a DIYer, you're certainly entitled to do so! What we'd really like is for the book to be an inspiration, or motivation, something to give you a few ideas that might make you say, "Hey, I could do something like that!"

Something for Everyone

We tried to include variety in the projects, both in purpose and scope. Some of the projects—the barn quilt, for instance—are large and somewhat complex. Others—like the old-fashioned log jack or the goat seesaw—can probably be completed in an afternoon. We aimed for diversity in the skill levels and time required, so there is something for everyone here.

Why DIY?

But hang on a minute—why even DIY at all? As we said, self-reliance is almost a part of the farmer's job description, but if anyone reading this is still asking, we'll offer a few more reasons:

1. IT SAVES MONEY

There's no question that building and constructing items from your own materials is usually a money-saver. Sure, you might be able to purchase a set of sawhorses, or a rabbit nest box, or even a beehive from a catalog or at the local home improvement store, but it's almost certainly cheaper to build these items yourself, particularly if you already have the lumber or materials on hand. Putting materials that you might already own (maybe scraps from other projects around the farm!) to use not only gets them out of the barn or shed, it turns them into a useful product in exchange for a little effort. (Farmers tend to hang on to odds and ends and scraps of lumber. We're not saying *we* have any experience with this, of course . . .)

2. UNIQUENESS

While you might be able to find a goat milking stand for sale, it's a large item that will likely be expensive, especially if you have to ship it. But you'd be hard-pressed to find a fence post stone crib for sale, or a stone boat, in the local classifieds. Building your own projects—like rabbit tractors, livestock medicine cabinets, or display stands for your farmers' market produce— allows you to construct items for your farm that you probably won't easily find anywhere else. Plus, it allows you to customize the projects and put your own spin on them, tweaking the dimensions or functions to suit your farm's specific needs.

3. FUN AND SATISFACTION

Finally, we think there's a lot of satisfaction to be had in building for yourself. It's that self-reliance again—there's just something to be said for being able to meet a need on your own. Also, these projects can be fun! We truly enjoyed designing and building these items, and we hope you do, too. Take your time, and stay safe.

Now then—off to work!

How to Read the Cut List

This column shows the dimensions of the piece(s) you'll end up with after cutting them from the lumber.

This is the type of lumber you'll need to source.

This is how many pieces of lumber you'll have after you make the cut(s).

CUT LIST

• 2	2 ft. (61 cm)	2×6s
• 1	16 in. (40.6 cm)	2×6
• 1	22 ½ (57 cm)	2×6
• 2	5 ½ in. (140 mm)	2×4 blocks
• 1	3 ft. (91.4 cm)	1×2 or 2×2 (for lever)
• 2	2 ft. (61 cm)	2×12s
• 1	2 ft. (61 cm)	2×4

About Metric Conversions

Lengths of lumber are sold, in North America, by their nominal dimensions, which are usually different from their actual dimensions. For example, a 2×4 actually measures 1½ × 3½ inches. For lumber like this, the metric conversions reflect the nominal rather than the actual dimensions.

1×1	=	25 × 25 mm
1×2	=	25 × 51 mm
1×6	=	25 × 152 mm
1×8	=	25 × 203 mm
2×2	=	51 × 51 mm
2×4	=	51 × 101 mm
2×6	=	51 × 152 mm
2×12	=	51 × 305 mm
4×4	=	101 × 101 mm

1×6

2×4

4×4

1×8

While this is not an exhaustive listing of all the tools you may require for these projects, here's a quick rundown of the basic tools needed for many of the projects, as well as a few thoughts about using them.

Carpentry Tools

Electric Drill

Modern lithium-ion battery-powered electric drills are wonderfully versatile tools. In addition to their usefulness in drilling holes through wood, electric drills also double as fantastic electric screwdrivers, making short work of framing tasks and chores that involve fastening larger pieces of lumber, like 2×4s and the like. In fact, we'd go so far as to say that quickly fastening screws is really what cordless drills are most useful for.

Choosing an electric drill is a matter of power vs. weight/size. A smaller, lighter cordless drill might be nicer to carry and easier to handle, but may not possess the power of a larger drill (although this isn't necessarily true). Likewise, a robust drill will probably be stronger, but possibly more expensive, too. Generally speaking, a drill lighter than about 12 volts might be a little too weak for the workload required by some of these projects.

Whatever type of cordless drill you choose, you might consider obtaining two batteries for it. That way, when one of them runs low, you don't have to stop working—you can charge one battery while you continue to work with the other one. Also, be sure to pick up a good selection of screw bits in various sizes, including Phillips, square, and torque bits, as well as various sizes of hole-drilling bits.

Circular Saw

No true DIYer should be without one. The circular saw is often the workhorse of many garages, workshops, and jobsites, and you'll definitely want one on hand for the projects in this book. Circular saws are available in both traditional plug-in varieties that generally have more power, and smaller portable battery-powered kinds. These battery-powered versions can be handy indeed, but may not have the power you need to accomplish some tasks quickly enough. Circular saws have small round blades—7¼ in. (184 mm) is a common diameter—that are capable of most crosscutting straight and miter cuts, and they can make rip cuts, too.

Miter Saw

Need to make many short crosscuts in a hurry? Are you looking for a quick way to cut multiple long pieces of lumber into shorter sections? Or perhaps you need to make a few precise angled (mitered) cuts? A miter saw might be just what you need for your woodworking setup. While not always specifically essential—you can probably get away with using your circular saw for the same jobs—a miter saw will definitely speed up your workflow and make these tasks easier.

Jigsaw

Not used all that often for basic construction work, a jigsaw is nevertheless essential for certain specific tasks, when making a very precise cut—particularly a curved cut—is what's needed. It's definitely a tool that is worth having around in the workshop for projects like those in this book. Besides wood, some jigsaws can be used for cutting mild steel, aluminum, or plastics. Naturally, a more powerful jigsaw—one over five amps—will have an easier time cutting through heavy materials, and may also have extra features. When shopping, consider purchasing a jigsaw with orbital action (this helps the blade cut more effectively) and variable speed so that you can speed up or slow down the blade as needed while making turns. Cordless battery-powered jigsaws are available, but may be less powerful than corded versions and weigh more.

Table Saw

When it comes to cutting wood, most people are probably more familiar with circular saws, miter saws, or even handsaws. Even though they work in different ways, these saws all have one thing in common: they work by *crosscutting*, that is, by cutting the wood across the grain, usually in fairly short distances. To take a very simple cut, for example, imagine cutting an 8 ft. (244 mm) 2×4 down to 6'. To do this only requires a fairly short cut across the short end of the 2×4. This cut goes across the wood's grain (a crosscut), and is easily and quickly accomplished by a circular saw, chop saw, or handsaw.

Now consider the table saw, which works under a different concept. Instead of being used to make relatively short cuts across the grain, a table saw is capable of making long *rip cuts*—cuts parallel to the grain of the wood. For example, a table saw could

Performing a rip cut with the table saw

be used to modify an 8 ft. (244 mm) 2×4 into two 8 ft. (244 mm) 2×2s, or some similar type of cut, and it can do this very quickly and effectively, providing pro-quality results with minimal effort on the part of woodworker. However, a table saw is a large, expensive tool, so you may or may not have easy access to one. Luckily, in a pinch, your circular saw can also make rip cuts with the use of a *rip guide*, but this isn't as easy to do and your cuts might not be quite as straight as they would be with a table saw. If you do need to perform a lot of rip cuts, a table saw is definitely the way to go.

Squares

A ruler-like tool that is quite un-squarelike itself, a square is an invaluable carpentry tool that can be used for a variety of purposes, but it's especially good at keeping your construction projects, well, square. There are two types of squares we suggest you have on hand: framing squares and triangle

Framing square

Triangle square

squares. Framing squares are "L"-shaped and very useful for keeping right angles perfectly at 90°, especially when constructing larger items out of long pieces of lumber. Triangle squares are very helpful as simple quick rulers for making cut lines, but they also help you easily mark angled cut lines for angles other than 90°. Triangle squares are light and compact, and easily fit in a pocket or tool belt while you work.

Tape Measure

One tool that is absolutely necessary for proper construction of almost all the projects in this book is a good tape measure. Because you'll be using it so often, we recommend looking for a quality tape measure that will hold up to frequent use and is easy to use. Find one with a locking mechanism that you like; different tapes use different types of levers or buttons to lock the tape and you'll want one that you find intuitive. Also, if you're not already a frequent carpenter, take a minute or two to familiarize yourself with the inch fraction markings on the tape. There are different-sized lines to make different-sized fractions easy to find at a glance, including half inch, quarter inch, eighth inch, and sixteenth inch.

Essential marking tools that work together: tape measure, triangle square, pencil

It might not seem like an eighth or a sixteenth inch might make much of a difference, but you would be surprised how critical these small amounts can be in the world of carpentry. Finally, select a tape that is the length you like best: 25 ft. (7.62 meters) is a fairly standard size, but you can also find smaller 16 ft. (4.87 meter) tapes that should also be sufficient for the projects in this book.

Hammer

For many basic construction tasks, we will often recommend a cordless drill and screws for assembly, just because it makes the job so easy. Still, a good hammer is an essential tool to have around for several reasons. Besides its basic use as a nailer—a job which a good hammer and a practiced arm can make quick work of—hammers are constantly needed for the gentle tapping or positioning of tight joints, or for carefully pulling out bent or misplaced nails or staples. Hey—mistakes happen!

For basic construction and for the projects outlined in this book, our advice is to select a standard claw hammer—perfect for nailing and occasional pulling or prying. Try a 16-ounce (453 gram) hammer as an excellent balance of weight and performance.

Wood Glue and Wood Clamps

Some carpentry projects will benefit from the addition of wood glue to help secure joints. The additional bond provided by the glue, in addition to the standard screws or nails, can help make your project extra strong. Along with glue, you'll also find that wood clamps are handy to hold wood in place while you fasten it, or to hold something down while the wood glue dries. Having a few different sizes and lengths of wood clamps on hand is probably a good idea.

Applying wood glue

Holding glued surfaces together with clamps

Finish Nailer

Some of the projects will be sped up considerably with the use of a pneumatic finish nailer. These nailers can fasten wood extremely quickly and make it look great at the same time. Obviously, the use of a finish nailer also demands that you obtain an air compressor to go with it. We understand that not everyone will have access to a finish nailer, but if you do, this is a good way to go.

Pencil

While you can of course use any basic pencil for marking measurements on your lumber, you'll find that a pencil made specifically for carpentry is a benefit. These pencils are generally thicker than regular pencils, so they have the ability to make bolder marks on lumber. Also, you might find that using a flat pencil rather than a round one is beneficial in keeping the pencil from constantly rolling off your worktable or sawhorses.

Razor Knife

Razor knives are one of those construction tools that are just convenient to have around. You can't ever be sure exactly when you'll want one, but when the need arises, it's a tool that's very handy to have on hand. Obviously, razor knives are extremely sharp and care must be taken whenever handling them.

Level (Spirit Level)

Whether you select a longer 3 or 4 foot (91 or 122 cm) version, or you stick with a simple (and inexpensive) 1 or 2 foot (30 or 60 cm) style, a good level is a highly valuable tool to keep in your carpentry toolbox. Levels couldn't be simpler to use—simply lay the level down against a flat surface on the project you're working on, and the convenient small bubble inside the glass window will show you precisely how accurate—or inaccurate!—your level surface is. Levels can also be utilized vertically, to verify if something is *plumb*—the vertical equivalent of level.

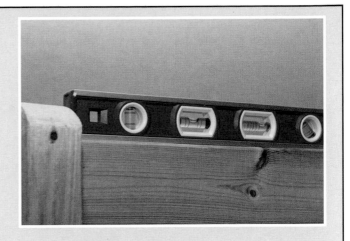

Sawhorses

Trust us—you'll want a set of sawhorses for all your carpentry work. In fact, you'll want several sets—they're just so convenient, whether you're cutting wood or simply in need of a table-like workspace for all of your project materials. Luckily, we show you how to make your own sawhorses (on pages 92–97), so you can build as many sets as you need!

GENERAL SAFETY WARNING

It goes without saying that any activity involving construction and assembly using hand or power tools should be approached with due caution and safety in mind, and these DIY projects are no exception. Always use caution when working on any construction project—safety should always be the main priority. Pay attention to your task and your surroundings, including curious onlookers. Read manuals and learn the safest ways to operate your tools, and don't ever place yourself in danger while working. Many of the activities detailed in this book have the potential to be dangerous, and failure to exercise proper safety behaviors could result in injury or death. The authors and publisher cannot assume responsibility for any damage to property or injury to persons or property as a result of the use or misuse of the information provided.

Non-Carpentry Tools

Not every project in this book is specifically a
carpentry project—this is a farming book after all, so
naturally we included some farming projects! Here are
a few additional tools you'll want on hand for these.

Shovels/Spades/Digging Tools

Digging a hole is a key step for projects like planting
a fruit tree, so you'll need some quality digging
tools. While it's possible you have a tractor or skid-
steer loader with an attachment large enough for
these jobs, we'll assume that most readers will be
approaching these tasks via the means of the more
labor-intensive but far less expensive shovel. But
just because you're doing it by hand doesn't mean
the chore has to be unpleasant. A new round-tipped
shovel with a quality and—this is important—sharp
blade, will help you make quick work of all kinds of
digging and shoveling tasks—even chopping through
thick sod!

   Don't forget to also keep on hand a square-head
shovel—properly known as a *spade*. These tools
are great for generally moving soil around, but
also to smooth out, fine-tune, and just generally
"square" a digging site. We also would recommend a
long—perhaps six-foot (two-meter)—*digging bar* for
loosening rocks and soil. One more tool? Add a *steel
rake* to your arsenal, perfect for smoothing out soil
and removing rocks.

Spade and shovel

Steel rake

Digging bar

Paintbrushes/Rollers

Need some paint to put the finishing touch on a project? Or perhaps the whole project depends on paint—like the barn quilt? Paintbrushes and rollers to the rescue. Roller handles with disposable/replaceable roller ends are cost-effective and easy because you can simply throw out the spent roller at the end of the day. For paintbrushes, keep a few various widths on hand so that you have the right one for the right job. Also, choose a paintbrush bristle material that will work well with the type of paint or stain you're using.

Paint roller and tray

Paintbrush

Wire Snips/Tin Snips

Hardware cloth and welded wire fencing are very useful products and are more durable than, say, chicken wire. Both products are easy to cut with large tin snips, or a smaller wire snip. However, hardware cloth and welded wire can be somewhat challenging to work with, as the cut sections can be very sharp, and because it often tries to return to its "memory" position, especially if it was stored on a roll. For these reasons, its best to have a helper on hand when you're preparing and cutting these products with the snips, and be sure to wear gloves and eye protection.

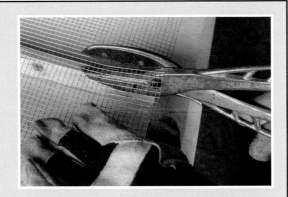

Staple Gun

Hand in hand with hardware cloth goes a staple gun to hold down the wire. Staple guns are excellent tools because they're easy to use, inexpensive, and effective. We highly recommend them.

Safety Gear

Work smart—keep your safety glasses, ear protection, dust mask, and other safety items at hand and use them every time they're needed. No DIY project is fun unless it's safe, and safety gear is critical. Also, wear proper gloves when needed for some tasks—they can make handling lumber easier on your hands, for example. Keep some extra safety gear handy for anyone who wants to help (or watch)! Also: get help if you need it. Sometimes having a more experienced DIYer around to help explain something or lend a hand can make the project more fun and more successful.

PROJECTS

Page	PROJECT NAME	SKILL LEVEL	TIME REQUIRED
18	Build a Bee House	Advanced	3 or more hours
26	Make a Candy Board for Honey Bees	Intermediate	2 hours
32	Extract and Bottle Honey	Advanced	3 or more hours
38	Build a Goat Seesaw	Intermediate	3 or more hours
44	Build a Log Jack	Intermediate	3 or more hours
50	Paint a Barn	Advanced	3 or more hours
54	Plant a Fruit Tree	Intermediate	2 hours
61	Protect a Fruit Tree	Easy	1 hour
67	Build a Rabbit Nest Box	Intermediate	1 hour
71	Build Sawhorses	Easy	1 hour
75	Build a Stone Boat	Intermediate	2 hours
80	Build a Stone Crib	Intermediate	2 hours
84	Build a Beehive	Advanced	3 or more hours
93	Build a Goat Stand	Advanced	3 or more hours
101	Build a Farmers' Market Display Stand	Advanced	3 or more hours
108	Build a Rabbit Tractor	Advanced	3 or more hours
117	Make Cottage Cheese	Intermediate	1 hour
121	Build a Barn Quilt	Advanced	3 or more hours
130	Graft a Fruit Tree	Intermediate	1 hour
134	Build a Barn/Stable Medicine Cabinet	Intermediate	3 or more hours

KEY

SKILL LEVEL:
- Easy
- Intermediate
- Advanced

TIME REQUIRED
- 🕙 1 hour
- 🕙🕙 2 hours
- 🕙🕙🕙 3 or more hours

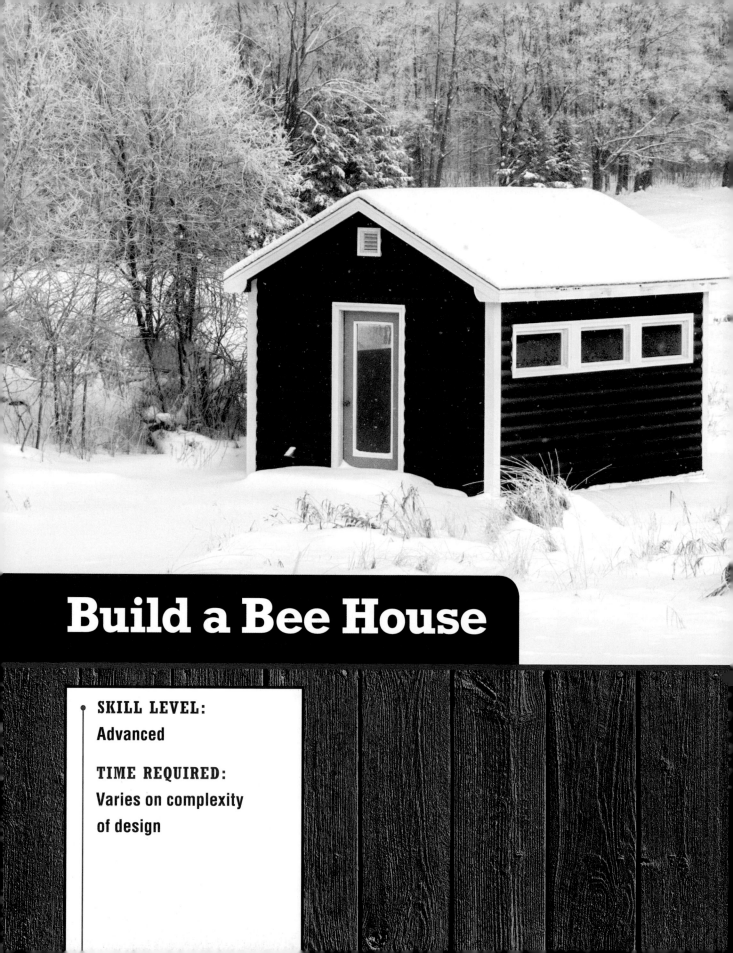

Build a Bee House

SKILL LEVEL:
Advanced

TIME REQUIRED:
Varies on complexity
of design

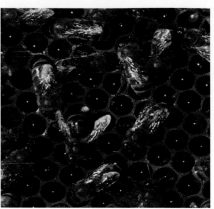

When you make the decision to move into livestock farming, you're also taking on the responsibility of building and maintaining the housing required to keep animals warm and safe. Whether it's a chicken coop, or a three-sided shed to provide horses or cattle with a wind break, or even a full-scale barn for sheep or goats, providing adequate shelter for animals is one of the major tasks for a livestock farmer—and often one of the most expensive investments in keeping livestock. But wait—what if you're a *beekeeper*? Beehives are kept outside all the time—does that let you off the hook on the shelter topic?

Well, maybe, but maybe not. Beehives are usually kept outdoors without much protection from the weather. Many beekeepers shelter their bees simply by providing a location out of the wind, a coat of paint to protect the wood, a heavy rock on top to pin down the outer cover, and a string of electric fence to discourage predators. And this can work fine in some circumstances. But there are a few problems with this method. First of all, electric fencing only goes so far in discouraging predators. Smaller animals like skunks or raccoons (both of which prey on beehives) may slip under or through the fencing. Electric fencing might discourage larger predators like black bears for a time, but if a bear ever does get a taste of honey from the hives, he may be impossible to stop next time, fencing or not.

Cold winters are another factor. Bees have a natural defense against cold temperatures—they form a cluster within the interior of the hive, where the outside bees rapidly "shiver" by working their wing muscles rapidly. This activity generates enough heat to keep the interior of the cluster at an amazing 90°F (32°C); the bees constantly take turns resting on the inside of the cluster and warming up the outside, except for the queen, who remains in the center of the cluster. However, it's critical that the humidity inside the hive remain low, as too much moisture can condense on the hive's interior and begin to drip on the bees, which may freeze them to death. Long periods of cold where the bees are unable to fly is another challenging factor. Personally speaking, these are major problems for us, given the length and severity of our northern Wisconsin winters. But even folks with shorter winters may experience difficulty in overwintering bees.

Because of both of these problems—predators and cold winters—we decided that our bees needed to be housed in a more permanent structure. We call ours "The Bee House," but you may hear of similar structures described as "bee sheds." Besides protecting the bees, we also use ours for handy storage of our beekeeping supplies and extra hive boxes.

What we'd like to do here is present the *concept* of a bee house project, and show you what we did. We're not going to dive into specific instructions, or even include a cut list or tool list. What we are going to do is show you a complete breakdown of our build, and try to show some of our thought processes and decision-making as we worked through the construction. Think of this as an inspiration—or a jumping-off place—for your own bee house/bee shed project.

STEP-BY-STEP

1 **SITE SELECTION AND FOUNDATION.** When evaluating and choosing the construction site for our bee house, we considered most of the same attributes that one would normally consider when siting a regular beehive in North America: we chose an area with excellent southeastern exposure (so that the rising sun quickly warms the hives and helps the bees get an early start), good soil drainage, and some protection against the prevailing western winds. Our bee house sits next to some small trees that provide wind protection as well as shade on hot, sunny summer afternoons. Additionally, the bee house is in a field that naturally grows early spring dandelions, and is not far from some flowering fruit trees, for an easy nectar source.

Once we chose the exact location, we began the site ground preparation. The spot we chose was naturally level, but still required some ground work to lower certain high points and raise low spots. Then we hauled in materials to begin construction.

2 **PREPARE THE FOUNDATION.** We chose 12 × 16 ft. (365 × 487 cm) as the dimensions of our bee house's footprint. While these dimensions make for a substantial building and present a fairly large construction undertaking for a DIYer, this size nevertheless doesn't require a formal foundation to carry the load, which saves time and cost. Setting cinder blocks directly on the prepared ground was enough here, but time and care had to be taken to ensure the blocks were all the same height—a transit is invaluable for making the precise adjustments needed. Short pieces of treated lumber of varying thicknesses can also be used as shims to achieve the correct spacing. Then we tied together the overall shape of the foundation and made sure everything was perfectly square.

Transit

3   CONSTRUCT THE SUBFLOOR. We used treated 4x4s—thirteen of them—on 16 in. (40 cm) centers as the floor joists for our bee house, sitting on top of the larger timbers of the foundation. This provided us with a very strong floor to support the weight above. We then used 1×6s to create a subfloor decking.

4   FRAME THE WALLS. Framing out the four walls—each one built separately as a complete piece—is no problem for an experienced carpenter. This process, even though it looks complex, isn't terribly difficult. However, the framed walls can be quite heavy and it required several people to get the walls to the site and raise them vertically (we built the frame of each wall back at the shop). To help keep costs down on this project, we were able to reuse a large amount of unused lumber from other projects.

STEP-BY-STEP

5 **ADD HEADERS.** Also needed were two larger headers to go atop the longer (16 ft. [487 cm]) walls— again, we needed a few helpers on hand to raise these headers. We also insulated the interiors of the headers for added warmth in the winter—the rest of the bee house was insulated later on in the process.

6 **ADD TRUSSES.** The roof of your bee house could be a traditional roof, as we show here, or you could choose a kind of barn-inspired gambrel roof. For our traditional shed look, we were able to lower construction costs by repurposing trusses from a different project. A little modification was all that was needed to make them work well here. With the walls up and the trusses in place, the true outline of the bee house began to take shape.

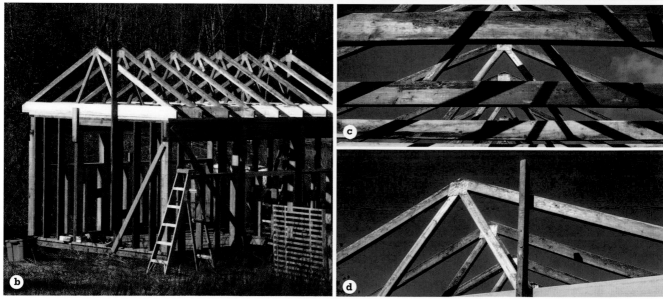

7 ROOFING. No matter how small the building—even a little bee shed—safety during construction is always paramount, especially when working on the roof. After installing the roof underlayment (providing a moisture barrier), we began adding shingles. Using a chalkline to make straight horizontal lines on the underlayment can help you keep your shingles straight.

8 INSTALL WINDOWS. One of our goals was to have a great deal of natural light in the bee house. If you're near enough to a power source, it's of course possible to wire your bee house with electricity for working lights. (We actually wired ours for possible future solar power, but our site itself is too far from a power source and so is effectively "off-grid.") Instead, we planned for three large windows along both long sides to bring in plenty of morning and afternoon light.

9 INSTALL THE DOOR. We framed the front of the bee house so that it would hold a standard-size service door. Then we selected one that was mostly glass to allow in additional light from the south.

10 ADD HOUSEWRAP. Remember, besides providing safety from predators, one of the key purposes of the bee house is to lower humidity in the winter. Adding housewrap under the siding was one important step in getting to that goal, as it provides a barrier between the weather outside and the interior of the bee house, where all of the hives will be kept.

11 ADD SIDING. Naturally, we don't want to leave all that housewrap visible! Siding is the next step here; we went with a basic log siding to give the bee house a quaint cabin feel, but you could select any siding variety that you find appealing and that matches well with your property and the bee house's surroundings. We also installed gable vents on both gable ends to provide fresh air when the windows and door are shut.

12 LEAVE BEE ACCESS! Wait a minute—if the hives are going to be safe and sound *inside* the bee house, how will the bees get in and out of the hives? Simple! The hives will be placed with the front entrances facing the outer walls of the bee house. When attaching the siding, we simply left a narrow gap (you can see the light shining through the housewrap in the photo) that will line up perfectly with the hive entrances (we cut away the housewrap covering the gap later). This way the bees have direct access to the outdoors, but their hives are inside where predators and harsh weather can't reach.

13 PAINT. Painting isn't a difficult job, but it's time-consuming. Nevertheless, protecting the wood siding is critical for ensuring the long-term integrity of the bee house. We went with a basic "barn red" paint.

14 INSULATE. We used standard home insulation to insulate the walls and ceiling of the bee house. This helps control the temperature and humidity inside.

15 ADD FINISHING TOUCHES. To help cover up all that insulation and protect the subfloor, we used OSB (oriented strand board) to cover the entire interior of the bee house. We also placed stones along the foundation to make this area more attractive and prevent animals from crawling under the bee house.

Make a Candy Board
for Honey Bees

SKILL LEVEL:
Easy to intermediate

TIME REQUIRED:
Approximately 2 to 3
hours (not including the
hardening time required
for the finished candy)

Imagine this: It's deep winter. Outside, the growing snow depth has the world looking more wintry than a Currier & Ives print. Indoors, people snuggle down, waiting out winter in anticipation of spring.

And what about your bees? Hopefully, they've "battened down the hatches" and have formed their winter cluster to create warmth while they feed from their summer stores of honey.

CUT LIST

• 1	16¼ × 19⅞ in. (41 × 50.5 cm)	½ in. (13 mm) plywood (other thicknesses can work, too; just utilize whatever you have on hand.
• 2	14½ in. (36.8 cm)	¾ × 2 in. (19 x 51 mm) pine
• 2	19⅞ in. (50.5 cm)	¾ × 2 in. (19 x 51 mm) pine

(The measurements given here are intended to fit a standard ten-frame Langstroth hive. It's a simple matter to adjust the dimensions for an eight-frame hive if needed.)

PARTS LIST

• 3d or 4d galvanized box nails

If you farm in a cold, snowy region with long winters that can last into March (or beyond!) then you know how difficult it can be to overwinter a colony of bees successfully. In a perfect situation, your honey bees will still possess an ample supply of honey to carry them through the winter, even after you've harvested some for your own use. But what if winter runs a bit long? What if March comes in like a lion and stays that way? Or, suppose you unwittingly harvested more honey than you should have and the bees run out too soon?

Enter the candy board: an excellent insurance policy to guard against situations like these. Candy boards are a simple way for beekeepers to provide an additional—think of it as backup—food source for their honey bees during the winter months, giving the colonies an extra source of nourishment to help them survive. In northern regions, long winters are often the norm, and where we live we usually add them to our hives in November.

Preparing candy boards can make a fine project for a cozy afternoon, especially in late fall when you're happy to be working indoors anyway, away from the coming chill of winter. The work is interesting without being too difficult, and you'll feel good knowing that your bees will also be cozy and well-fed in their winter quarters.

TOOLS NEEDED

- Measuring tape
- Pencil
- Circular saw, chop saw, or table saw (a table saw can be helpful for cutting the plywood, but isn't required)
- Jigsaw
- Hammer
- Wood glue
- Framing square
- Large pot
- Candy thermometer
- Wooden spoon

CANDY RECIPE

- 2 cups (480 mL) sugar
- 1 bottle corn syrup (16 ounces [473 mL])
- 2 cups (480 mL) water
- ⅛ teaspoon (0.6 mL) cream of tartar

STEP-BY-STEP

1 **CUT ENTRANCE NOTCH.** Before you begin creating the frame of the candy board, you'll need to modify one of the 14½ in. (36.8 cm) pieces (what will become one of the short sides of the frame). Using a jigsaw, cut a simple 2 in. (51 mm) notch about ¼ in. (6 mm) deep, centered at 7¼ in. (184 mm): the total distance of the 2 in. (51 mm) notch therefore spans 6¼ to 8¼ in. (159 to 209 mm) on the 14½ in. (36.8 cm) board. This notch—small as it is—serves as an outside entrance for the bees.

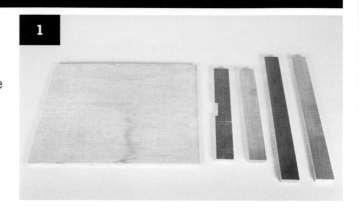

2 **ASSEMBLE THE CANDY BOARD FRAME.** Assembling the basic shape of the candy board frame is a fairly simple process. Essentially, all we have to do is build a rectangular frame using the long and short pine boards. To achieve the proper dimensions, be sure to place the shorter 14½ in. (36.8 cm) pieces *inside* the longer 19⅞ in. (50.5 cm) pieces. Prior to nailing, you can use a framing square if you'd like to help keep things straight, or you could even choose to construct the frame over your piece of plywood to ensure perfect 90° angles. We used just a hammer and galvanized nails for assembly here; of course you can choose to use an air nailer if you'd like. Pre-drilling pilot holes before hand nailing is another option to make things easier. When finished, the dimensions of your candy board frame should measure 16¼ × 19⅞ in. (41 × 50.5 cm).

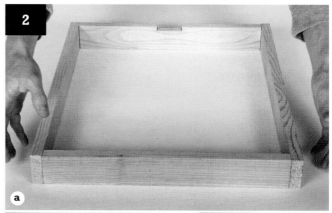

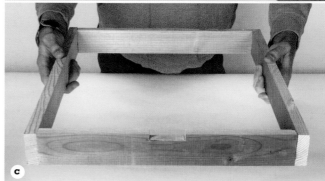

3 **ADD PLYWOOD BASE.** Next you can go ahead and actually fasten the plywood base to the frame. Put down a layer of wood glue first to help ensure a nice solid fit, and then use nails. Important: make sure that the notch you cut faces *opposite* the plywood base. Also, take care to make the seam between the plywood and the frame tight and secure so that none of the candy will leak out. That's all there is to building the actual candy board; now you can move on to preparing the candy mixture.

4 **PLAN YOUR RECIPE.** You'll discover that there are many recipe variations for making honey bee candy. Some recipes call for corn syrup, others omit corn syrup and exchange it with honey or merely additional sugar. Some recipes suggest vinegar; others do not. Finally, some beekeepers prefer adding in a pollen substitute. We've experimented with various recipes and have found that this one—listed on page 33—works well for us:

5 **PREPARE THE CANDY MIXTURE.** On the stove in a large pot, combine the sugar, corn syrup, water, and cream of tartar. Stir the mixture while you heat it, until the candy thermometer reads 240° Fahrenheit (115° Celcius). It will likely take about 20 to 25 minutes for the candy to reach the target temperature. When it does, remove the pot from the heat and allow the mixture to sit until it cools down to 180° Fahrenheit (82° Celcius); the cooling time is about 45 minutes). When the candy reaches this temperature, renew stirring and continue to beat for about 10 minutes or until the mixture thickens and becomes cloudy.

6 **ADD CANDY TO BOARD.** At this point, immediately transfer the mixture from the pot to the candy board frame (be careful—the pot will be heavy and hot!) by pouring the candy mixture directly onto the plywood. Avoid filling the candy board completely—leave at least ½ in. (13 mm) of space down from the top edge of the frame.

Then take a break and wait. The candy hardening process will likely take several hours (or even overnight) before the candy board will be dried and hard enough to add to your hive. You'll know the board is ready when the candy has turned from clear to white and is completely hard (not sticky or gooey).

7 INSTALL THE CANDY BOARD ON THE HIVE. Installing the finished candy board is a simple matter. Just visit your hive during good weather conditions and at a time of day that is suitable for bee work and replace the hive's standard inner cover with the new candy board. Orient with the candy facing down, and then return the outer cover to its normal position. (Alternatively, leave the inner cover in place and position your new candy board between it and the frames below). Task complete! Your honey bees now have an extra food source to help see them through those final tough weeks of winter.

Extract and Bottle Honey

SKILL LEVEL:
Advanced

TIME REQUIRED:
Approximately 5 hours

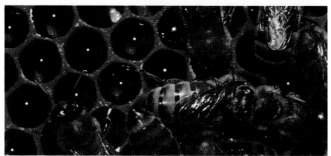

The hobby farmer with limited property—maybe only a handful of acres or less—may think she's in for a tough challenge to find a type of livestock that she can raise properly on such limited space. Likewise, a newcomer to farming might be very interested yet intimidated by the prospect of keeping livestock. In both of these cases, chickens are often put forth as a good option—relatively easy to care for and not requiring immense infrastructure or acreage. While we love chickens, too—in fact, we wrote an entire book of DIY chicken projects—we'd like to step outside the box for a moment and suggest another type of "livestock" that is wonderful for beginners and doesn't require a huge investment to get started: honey bees.

PARTS LIST	TOOLS NEEDED
• Frames of honey!	• Bee escape/fume board
	• Uncapping knife
	• Uncapping fork
	• Uncapping tank
	• Honey extractor
	• Strainer
	• Honey collection bucket
	• Bottles/jars

(It should go without saying—but we will say it nonetheless—that all of the tools and equipment that come into contact with your honey need to be perfectly clean prior to use! This includes all the items on this list except for the bee escape or fume board.)

Honey bees make wonderful livestock. They require time and attention—but not in the same "twice a day, every day" way that say, cows or goats (or even chickens) do. Caring for honey bees can be more relaxed and seasonal (for example, there isn't a whole lot to do for them in the winter, short of supplying a candy board—see page 30). Still, there is plenty of work to do keeping bees, and you'll have ample opportunity to enjoy the satisfaction of caring for living creatures who depend on you—the same as any other livestock. And of course, there is the honey.

Obtaining homemade honey sourced from your own bees and your own property is probably the biggest reason people get into bees (other reasons include garden and crop pollination and byproducts like wax). So, for that reason, we thought it would be beneficial to include an overview of the basic steps involved in actually collecting and bottling the honey that your bees put so much effort into making. It sounds so simple—just put the honey into bottles, right?—but there are a lot of components to this process and a few things (like removing the honey from the hives) that require precision. Every situation can be slightly different, but we aim to provide a solid overview of the process.

It's important to realize that you won't be able to harvest honey until after the bees have had all spring and summer to gather nectar and create a surplus of honey. Your bees will need a certain amount of honey to see them through the winter, so in order for them to survive over the winter, you'll need to wait to harvest honey until they've created enough honey for themselves *and* extra for you. How much honey you need to leave in the hive depends on your climate— longer winters mean the bees need more honey to see them through—but expect them to need somewhere from fifty to more than a hundred pounds of honey. Weaker colonies may need to be left with all of their honey in order for them to survive over winter. When strong colonies who have stored excess honey in the upper portions of the hive (the "supers") are ready for a honey harvest, following are the steps to reaping your reward.

STEP-BY-STEP

1 **REMOVE THE SUPERS FROM THE HIVE.** Ideally, the bees will have kept the upper supers (where the excess honey is stored) separate from the brood. Some beekeepers use "queen excluders"—essentially a type of screen that allows workers to pass through but keeps out the larger queen—to ensure this. Assuming that the desired super only contains capped honey, the first step is to remove any worker bees from the super. There are two options here: the fast method is to utilize a fume board to quickly repel any worker bees out of the super and encourage them down into the deep hive boxes. However, this method can sometimes cause many bees to completely evacuate the hive. The second, slower method is to use a "bee escape." A bee escape is a "maze" of sorts that is added below the supers about a day or two before the honey harvest is scheduled. Worker bees can easily leave the upper supers and make their way into the lower portions of the hive, but they will have difficulty finding their way back up. In this way, the honey supers will be free of workers with only a little effort, but the process takes longer. No matter which method you use, once the honey supers are free of bees, you can remove them from the hive and take the precious frames to your honey bottling room for the next step.

2 UNCAP THE FRAMES.

Worker bees place wax seals or "caps" over honey cells for long-term storage, and these caps will need to be removed before you can extract the honey from the frames (harvesting uncapped honey isn't recommended). To do this, use your uncapping knife to slowly and carefully cut along the edges of the frames—a slow, sawing motion usually helps. The job will be easier if you use an electric (heated) uncapping knife. Your uncapping fork (or "scratcher") can then be used to further fine-tune the uncapping process. If you uncap the frames while using an uncapping tank to catch the caps, the resulting beeswax can be put to use later in beeswax products and crafts.

STEP-BY-STEP

3 EXTRACT THE HONEY FROM THE FRAMES. As each frame of honey is uncapped, it can be placed vertically into your extractor. The extractor is essentially a stainless steel drum (occasionally plastic on less-expensive models) with an internal cage to hold frames of honey, and a hand crank or motor for rapidly rotating the cage. Hand-crank extractors are less expensive but a real workout to use; motorized extractors are nice but cost more. In either case, the rapid spinning of the cage creates enough centrifugal force to empty the honey out of the frames, where it drips down the sides of the extractor and out the gate at the bottom.

4 STRAIN AND COLLECT THE HONEY. As the honey drains out of the extractor's gate, it is caught in a food-grade five-gallon bucket that also has a gate at the bottom. But as the honey is collected, it's very important that a strainer is used to prevent unwanted debris from entering the collection bucket. Straining can greatly slow down your extracting process, but it is nevertheless a critical step in ensuring a quality finished product.

5

BOTTLING. After allowing the honey to settle in the collection bucket for a time, you can begin the process of bottling it into (clean!) jars. This job isn't difficult but requires care and patience as it is a slow process, plus you're creating a food product so doing a good job and keeping everything very clean is of the utmost importance. To start bottling, simply set the five-gallon honey bucket on a table or other elevated position and hold an open empty honey jar directly under the bucket's gate. Carefully and slowly open the gate—you can control the flow rate of the honey by adjusting the size of the hole—and collect honey into the jar until it's full (don't overfill into the neck area of the bottle). Don't allow honey to drip over the edges. Finally, attach the lid and seal the jar.

Some folks use glass jars for their honey; others use plastic. Glass jars are perhaps more traditional, and possibly healthier in that there is no possibility of plastic leaching into the honey; however, glass is heavy (for shipping) and can break. Plastic is light and less breakable, even squeezable for easy use, and comes in fun shapes. The choice is up to you.

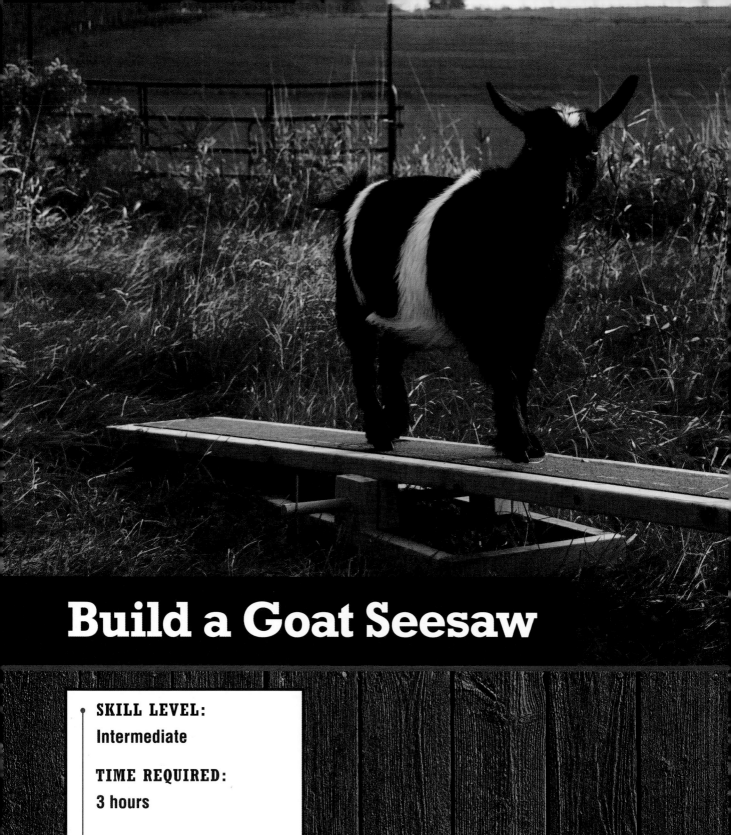

Build a Goat Seesaw

SKILL LEVEL:
Intermediate

TIME REQUIRED:
3 hours

If you have goats or have ever spent time around them, then you know that these rambunctious critters love to have fun, and one of their favorite ways to entertain themselves is to climb on things. Whether it's a result of their early origins in mountainous terrain or just their insatiable curiosity about all things new and exciting, goats love play structures of all varieties (although sometimes it seems that goats derive the most fun by pushing other goats *off* of these play structures!)

PARTS LIST	TOOLS NEEDED
• Box of 6 in. (152 mm) screws	• Circular saw
• Box of 3 in. (76 mm) screws	• Miter saw (optional, but makes the job easier)
• A few asphalt shingles	• Electric drill
• Box of short roofing nails or short screws	• ⅞ in. (22 mm) drill bit
	• Tape measure
	• Pencil
	• Square
	• Hammer (if using roofing nails)
	• Wood glue

CUT LIST

- 1   8 ft. (244 cm)   2×12
- 4   3½ × 3½ in. (89 × 89 mm)   2×4 blocks
- 2   24 in. (61 cm)   2×4s
- 2   14½ in. (36.8 cm)   2×4s
- 1   24 in. (61 cm)   ⅞ or 1 in. (22 or 25 mm) wooden dowel

This easy goat seesaw will provide plenty of entertainment for you and your goats. They'll cheerfully teeter-totter up and down, and the added traction of the shingles helps to minimize worries of slipping.

We recommend always supervising your goats as they play on their seesaw, especially if you have young goats that might be small enough to lay down underneath it.

STEP-BY-STEP

1 MAKE CUTS. The main component of the seesaw is an 8 ft. (244 cm) 2×12. If you purchase this board new from a lumberyard, be sure to measure it before using, as more than likely it won't be precisely 8 ft. but actually be a bit longer than that. Cut off any excess first, otherwise your seesaw might be unbalanced when you're finished. Take care especially when cutting 2×4s down to 3½ × 3½ in. (89 × 89 mm) blocks; use a longer 2×4 and a miter saw to keep your hands at a safe distance.

2 CONSTRUCT THE FEET. Begin by screwing one 3½ × 3½ in. (89 × 89 mm) block to the top of a 24 in. (61 cm) 2×4, as shown. It's important to get the spacing correct and accurately center the block on the 2×4. To help with this, make pencil marks on the 2×4 at 10¼ and 13¾ in. (260 and 349 mm). Use 6 in. (152 mm) screws to fasten the block to the 2×4, but take care to keep the screws away from the very center of the block, as we'll need to drill a hole there shortly. Repeat this step, so that you have two feet prepared.

3

DRILL HOLES. Now make a pencil mark in the center of each block. You can do this by measuring to 1¾ in. (44 mm) each way. Carefully drill a hole through the center of the block with your ⅞ in. (22 mm) drill bit. You should now have two sets of feet prepared, each with a hole in the blocks.

4

ADD BLOCKS TO THE SEESAW. Using 3 in. (76 mm) screws, you can now attach the remaining two 3½ × 3½ in. (89 × 89 mm) blocks to each side of the 2×12. To properly center the blocks, make pencil marks at 46¼ and 49¾ in. (117.5 and 126 cm). Use 3 in. (76 mm) screws to fasten.

5   **DRILL ADDITIONAL HOLES.** Now you'll need to drill two additional holes, each in the center of the block on the 2×12. Again use a ⅞ in. (22 mm) drill bit, and drill into marks at 1¾ × 1¾ in. (44 × 44 mm).

6   **ADD THE ROD AND FEET.** Insert the wooden dowel through the blocks on the 2×12, and then add the two feet you made in steps 1 and 2. It's easiest to build this upside-down, as shown. If your dowel seems loose, you can add wood glue to set it in place and keep it from moving from side to side; if it's fairly tight, you might not have to do this. If you'd like, you can shorten the dowel to 16 in. (40.6 cm).

STEP-BY-STEP

7 **COMPLETE THE STAND.** To finish off the seesaw's stand, use 3 in. (76 mm) screws to add the final two 14½ in. (36.8 cm) 2×4s to the ends of the feet. This forms a complete, sturdy stand that will support the seesaw properly.

8 **ADD SHINGLES.** We used a couple of asphalt shingles placed lengthwise along the top of the seesaw to help make the surface less slippery and give the goats something for their hooves to grip on. Another side benefit to this is that the shingles' rough surface can help wear down the goats' hooves if they play on it frequently. You can use short roofing nails to hold down the shingles, or you can use short screws.

9 **LET THE GOATS HAVE FUN!** Supervise your goats as you introduce them to the seesaw. Our goat, Dolly, jumped on immediately and seemed to enjoy the surprise of the seesaw's motion as she walked across it.

53

Build a Log Jack

SKILL LEVEL:
Intermediate

TIME REQUIRED:
3 hours

In some places across America, you'll still find farmers here and there working in traditional, old-fashioned ways. Sometimes it's a farmer who chooses to use draft horses for working fields and pulling wagons, or maybe it's a family putting up loose hay instead of baling it mechanically. Sometimes older-style tools are still put to good use: swinging a scythe instead of using a gas trimmer, choosing an axe instead of a chainsaw. Whether it's for a sense of nostalgia, self-sufficiency, or simply because tried-and-true methods can still get the job done, it can be a pleasure to work with old tools or in an old-fashioned way.

CUT LIST

- 2   2 ft. (61 cm)   2×6s
- 1   16 in. (40.6 cm)   2×6
- 1   22½ (57 cm)   2×6
- 2   5½ in. (140 mm)   2×4 blocks
- 1   3 ft. (91.4 cm)   1×2 or 2×2 (for lever)
- 2   2 ft. (61 cm)   2×12s
- 1   2 ft. (61 cm)   2×4

PARTS LIST

- 2   12 in. (305 mm)   11/16 in. (17 mm) conduit pieces
- 1   2 in. (51 mm) bull snap
- 1   removable chain link
- 1   5 ft. (152.4 cm) chain
- 1   4 in. (101 mm)   ¼ in. (6 mm) diameter screw hook
- 1   2 in. (51 mm)   ¼ in. (6 mm) diameter eye hook
- Box of 3 in. (76 mm) exterior screws
- Box of 6 in. (152 mm) exterior screws

To that end, we decided to show you how to build your own old-fashioned log jack. When sawing large logs into sections—whether today or a hundred years ago—it's usually helpful to have the log elevated. Not only does this save wear and tear on your back, but it speeds up the sawing process and prevents the saw blade from digging into the soil when you get down low in the log. Today, there might be several different options available for someone wanting to lift a log— but what did homesteaders do back before hydraulics and tractors? Well, one option that required just a little ingenuity and some simple construction is a log jack, and that's what we're looking at here. This log jack is made from just a few short pieces of lumber (it might be a great way to use up some scrap pieces you have around the farm) and is essentially a kind of large ratchet that allows you to slowly lift a heavy object, with little effort.

When completed, this log jack will indeed do its job of lifting and holding logs up for sawing, but we encourage prospective builders to view the project as a fun history lesson as much as a utilitarian device. We found it fascinating to learn how homesteaders a century or more ago used a clever device made out of very simple materials to do this job, and we hope that you do, too. This might make a nice group project to do with kids.

TOOLS NEEDED

- Circular saw
- Tape measure
- Pencil
- Two wood clamps
- Electric drill
- ⅞ in. (22 mm) drill bit
- ¼ in. (6 mm) drill bit
- Jigsaw

STEP-BY-STEP

1 **PREPARE FOR DRILLING.** A series of holes need to be drilled into both 2 ft. (61 cm) 2×6s to create the ratchet portion of the log jack. The holes need to be in identical positions on both 2×6s, so to make life easier and speed up the construction process, it's smart to temporarily clamp the two 2×6s together. Doing this means you'll only have to make one series of marks, and only drill one series of holes. It also ensures that the drilled holes will line up exactly on each 2×6, which will make the jack easier to use.

STEP-BY-STEP

2

DRILL HOLES. There should be two rows of holes running up the 24 in. (61 cm) 2×6s, with the centers of one row set in 1½ in. (38 mm) and the others centered at 4 in. (101 mm). For the height of the holes, one row should be drilled on *even* numbers: 4, 6, 8, 10, 12, 14, 16, 18, and 20 in. (101, 152, 203, 254, 305, 355, 406, 457, and 508 mm). The other row should be drilled on *odd* numbers: 3, 5, 7, 9, 11, 13, 15, 17, 19, and 21 in. (76, 127, 178, 228, 279, 330, 381, 432, 482, and 533 mm). The photos should help explain this a little better. Use a drill bit that is a little larger than your pieces of conduit—you want to make sure there will be plenty of play available between the conduit and the holes. For our ¹¹⁄₁₆ in. (17 mm) conduit, we used ⅞ in. (22 mm) drill bit. You'll be drilling multiple holes through a fairly thick amount of wood, so take care, and be sure your drill bit is sharp!

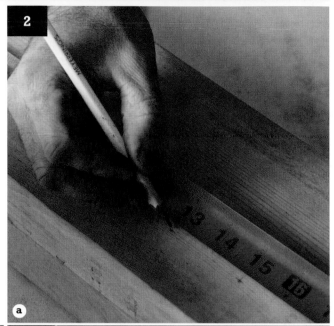

3 **CONSTRUCT THE RATCHET FRAME.** Now remove the clamps from the 2×6s. Next, use the 5½ in. (140 mm) 2×4 blocks as spacers between the two hole-filled 2×6s as shown, and secure with 6 in. (152 mm) screws. The entire width of the log jack is 6½ in. (165 mm), so 6 in. (152 mm) screws will create a very strong fit.

4 **BUILD THE BASE.** The ratchet section of the log jack will work better if it has a base to give it a little additional lift and help with stability. Take the two 2 ft. (61 cm) 2×12s and stand them upright, separated by the 2 ft. (61 cm) 2×4 as shown. Use 3 in. (76 mm) screws to fasten.

a

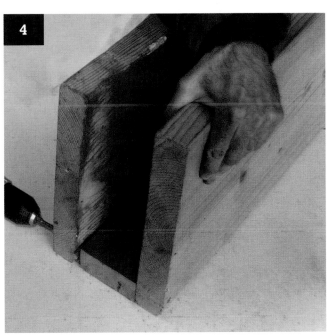

4

b

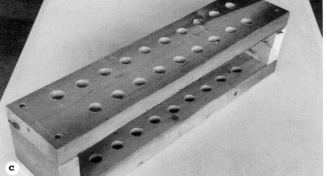

c

STEP-BY-STEP

5 **ATTACH THE BASE TO THE RATCHET.** Now set the ratchet upright on top of the base, flush with one end, and use more 3 in. (76 mm) screws to fasten the ratchet to the base. You'll need to screw in at an angle, as shown.

6 **BUILD THE SIDE STAND.** The log jack requires a side stand to hold up the other side of the chain that will lift the log. The side stand is extremely simple; using the shorter 16 in. (40.6 cm) 2×6 as a base, attach the 22½ in. (57 cm) 2×6 to the center of the 16 in. (40.6 cm) 2×6. You can easily find the center of the 16 in. (40.6 cm) base by making marks at 7¼ and 8¾ in. (184 and 222 mm). Attach the two pieces together with 3 in. (76 mm) screws.

7 **ADD A HOOK TO THE SIDE STAND.** You'll need to add a hook to the side stand to hold the chain; a robust 4 in. (101 mm) long, ¼ in. (6 mm) diameter screw hook will work, although the exact measurements of the hook aren't critical as long as it's strong enough to do the job. Use a ¼ in. (6 mm) drill bit first to create a pilot hole about 1½ in. (38 mm) down from the top of the side stand, then screw in the hook.

STEP-BY-STEP

8 **PREPARE THE LEVER.** Using a ¼ in. (6 mm) drill bit, prepare a hole in the short side of your 3 ft. (91.4 cm) lever, about 1 in. (25 mm) in from the end, then screw in the eye hook. Finally, use a jigsaw to cut two small notches in the lever, centered about 9½ and 12 in. (241 and 305 mm) from the end where you added the eye hook. These notches are essential for making the jack's lifting motion smooth and secure, and greatly eases the lifting process. On one end of the chain, attach a bull snap with a removable chain link; the bull snap attaches the chain to the lever.

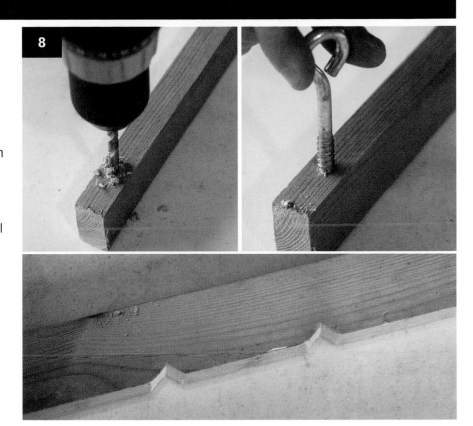

9 **PUT THE JACK TO WORK!** Now you can actually try out the jack. Place the ratchet on one side of the log and slip the chain under the log. Pull the slack tight, and attach the other end of the chain to the top of the side stand, which is placed on the opposite side of the log. To operate the jack, just follow this concise advice from a 1909 copy of the book *Handy Farm Devices and How to Make Them*, which describes a device similar to this one:

"By working the small end of the lever up and down and moving the pins up one hole at a time, a good-sized tree can be raised from the ground high enough to be sawed easily without a backache."

We found it rather fun to work the conduit pins up and down with the lever, and there's no doubt that it certainly makes raising the heavy log a simple process.

Paint a Barn

SKILL LEVEL:
Advanced

TIME REQUIRED:
Several days

What would the rural American landscape be without its iconic barns? No drive through the countryside is complete without barns standing proud over their farms' "amber waves of grain," and if you live on a farm of your own, chances are, there is a barn waiting for you each morning to work in. Modern barns may have metal siding that is extremely resilient and doesn't require much maintenance, but traditional wood structures—especially vintage barns—need the occasional fresh coat of paint over the course of their lifetimes in order to keep their wood protected and their appearance looking great. In the case of older barns in particular, fresh paint may be very important to ensuring that it remains a utilitarian building, useful for years to come. But what tools do you need to complete this job? What prep work needs to be done? Let's take a look at the multistep process and before you know it, your old barn will look like new again. (But your painting clothes? They'll never look new again . . .)

TOOLS NEEDED

- Paintbrushes
- Step ladder(s)
- Extension ladder(s)
- Drop cloths
- Caulk gun and caulk
- Paint sprayer and enough hoses to get the job done
- Pressure washer
- Masking tape
- Paint

1 **EVALUATE CONDITION AND REPAIR.** Before you run to the hardware or farming supply store and buy multiple gallons of "Barn Red" paint, stop and consider your barn's actual condition. Assuming that your barn is foundationally sound and satisfactorily "square" (if not, fixing these problems needs to be dealt with prior to painting), turn your attention to the actual walls you'll be painting. Thoroughly evaluate your barn's siding—is a coat of paint all that is required to restore the barn to top condition? Check for any broken or rotting areas of siding that might need replacement, then make any necessary repairs to ensure that your paint job won't go to waste on wood that won't last for years to come. Other things to consider replacing before painting include windows, window trim, vents, and doors. If they're all in good shape, continue on!

2 **REMOVE PAINT AND PREPARE.** The next step is pressure washing. This is important in order to remove all the remaining loose bits of paint, along with all the dust, dirt, cobwebs, and other debris (hey, it's a farm, right?) that might come between your paint and a clean surface on which it will stick. Depending on the size of your barn and your ladder skills, you might be able to do this job off of extension ladders, or you may choose to speed and ease up the process by borrowing or renting a cherry-picker truck. If there's any chance that some of the mist from the pressure washing can get inside the barn—perhaps through a vent or an upper-story window without glass—you might want to cover the openings with plastic before beginning. After the pressure washing process is completed, be sure to give your barn's wood plenty of time to dry out before moving on to painting. Areas of particularly thick paint—or spots you can't hit with the pressure washer—can be tackled with a paint scraper to help get down to the wood. Caulk any cracks or openings around windows, doors, and vents to create a good seal.

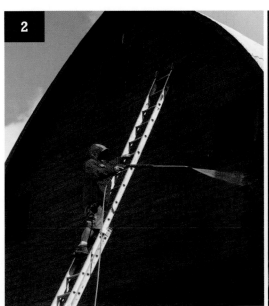

STEP-BY-STEP

OLD BARN? PROCEED WITH CAUTION!

If you suspect that your barn hasn't been painted since prior to 1978—the year that the production of lead paint was terminated—then there's a good chance that you may have a lead paint situation, in which case you'll need to have a professional remove the paint from the barn and properly dispose of the paint debris. Even if you're removing newer paint, there's still a possibility that older lead paint may remain underneath. You can test your barn's old paint with a lead paint test kit, but you should still wear a respirator if you're at all unsure.

3 **APPLY THE PAINT.** Depending on the type of paint you purchase and apply, you can expect 1 gallon (3.78 L) to cover approximately 300 square feet (27.87 m^2) of space, so a very large barn may require many gallons. Your paint's label may suggest a higher number, but aged barn wood will often absorb more paint than you expect, and in order to get good coverage you should figure on needing extra. Latex exterior paint is often recommended for applications like barns, although some paints also mix in a linseed-based oil for added durability. Many exterior paints are also self-priming, so think of the first coat as your "primer coat," and be sure to try to provide an even surface for the final coat to keep things looking great. (If you're attempting to paint very weathered wood that you've chosen not to replace, an oil-based paint will likely apply a bit better.)

You'll likely need to apply paint by hand for detail work such as around windows and doors, as well as on areas of rough wood where you really need to work the paint into. Paint rollers may or may not be helpful, depending on the type of wood. In many cases, a paint sprayer is essential for getting the job done in a timely and thorough fashion. Prior to spraying, be sure to mask off areas like windows, doors, vents, and roofing that you don't want to get damaged from overspray. One technique for making sure your paint really gets into the wood is to spray first to get the bulk of the paint applied and then to have someone come along behind you to work the paint into the wood by hand with a brush or roller. Again, these decisions will have to be made on a case-by-case basis, depending on the size and height of your barn, the time available, and the skills of the painter(s). Follow the paint manufacturer's recommendations for thinning, especially for latex-based paints, which are often thicker than oil-based paints and might need to be thinned slightly to prevent clogging in sprayers.

Once the first coat has dried (be patient!), apply the second coat, and then stand back and enjoy your "new" barn. Have fun during your painting project and remember: you're helping to preserve a little piece of history!

WHY RED?

While barns can be many colors—blue, green, white—it's the classic red barn that most people think of and expect when you say "vintage barn!" Prior to about 1790 or the early 1800s, however, American barns were typically not painted at all, and the wood was left completely natural. Then farmers began experimenting with paint as a way to protect the barn from the weather and make the wood last longer. Farmers then (and now?) were always on the lookout for ways to cut costs and save money, so they approached the idea of painting a barn from a utilitarian point of view, not a cosmetic one—as long as it got the barn protected, color wasn't a concern. Inexpensive paint recipes came into use, often including ingredients like linseed oil, lime, milk, and iron oxide (rust), which gave this early paint its now-famous red color. And that's how the red American barn was born, driven by simple economics.

c

d

Plant a Fruit Tree

SKILL LEVEL:

Intermediate

TIME REQUIRED:

2 hours

If you're tired of having a red thumb from misplaced hammer strikes during all these carpentry projects (that's a joke— hopefully it's not actually the case!), maybe you're ready to tackle a project that requires a green thumb instead.

Planting a fruit tree is a relatively simple project that can reap years of rewards. Not only will you be able to harvest fruit season after season (and depending on the eventual size of the tree, that could be a lot of fruit), you're also planting a future. It's not uncommon for fruit trees to live for decades, so it's quite possible that your children and grandchildren will someday enjoy the fruits of your labor, too.

TOOLS NEEDED

- Round-pointed shovel (or multiple shovels if you have help!)
- Tape measure
- Utility knife
- Steel rake
- Water container or hose

Broadly speaking, there are two common ways of planting fruit trees. The first is to plant bare-root specimens that arrive without leaves and, of course, without any soil surrounding their roots. This is the way mail-order trees are typically shipped and, when executed correctly, this can be the preferable approach, as the trees require less water and attention once planted.

But planting bare root trees is a bit more challenging (and, in the early days, less satisfying) than planting container-grown trees. Since they're actively growing in a soil-filled pot, these trees will have a full crown of leaves when purchased and can be considerably larger than their bare-root counterparts. The only problems? You'll have to find a local nursery that carries them, and either pick them up yourself or have them delivered. Plus, they require a lot of water after planting and are a little trickier to work with since the root ball and branches are heavy.

Still, the overall advantages offered by container-grown trees make them an ideal choice for the first-time orchardist. Planting them is straightforward, you don't have to fuss so much with positioning the roots, and—of no less importance—their larger starting size means they'll be closer to fruit production than bare root trees. You might even be able to plant trees that have already started producing fruit!

With this in mind, we'll focus our instructions on the planting of container-grown trees, though if you enjoy the process and want to expand your orchard plans, we encourage you to consider planting bare root trees as well.

STEP-BY-STEP

1 CHOOSE A LOCATION. Maybe you think your cute little fruit tree would look great growing right up alongside your house, but don't be fooled by the current size of your tree. You need to think long-term, and consider the size that the tree will reach once mature. If it's a standard-sized apple tree, you could be looking at a crown spread of at least twenty feet (six meters) plus a similar or greater height. Wherever you choose to plant your tree, be sure to give it plenty of room to grow and expand so that it won't be encroaching where it doesn't belong in ten years.

2

PREPARE THE HOLE. While it would be nice if you could dig a hole just large enough to fit the root ball, this really isn't the best for the tree. A better approach is to dig a hole two or three times the width of the root ball, which loosens up the surrounding soil and makes it easier for the roots to get properly established.

The depth of the hole should be carefully considered as well. Dig deeper than necessary at first so that you can backfill the bottom of the hole with loose material—again, to make it easy for the roots to get established. Once this loose material is in place, the hole should be deep enough so that the top of the root ball is level with or slightly lower than the surrounding ground level.

STEP-BY-STEP

3 REMOVE THE TREE FROM ITS POT. Depending on the size and weight of the root ball, you might find it easier said than done to remove the tree from its pot (which will typically be made of plastic). With a couple of people working carefully, you might be able to lift up the tree and pull the pot straight off, but if you're working alone (or if the tree is large and heavy), you're probably better off using a utility knife to slice open the pot.

If your tree did not come in a pot (some come packaged in burlap), follow essentially the same approach by cutting away and removing the burlap to free the root ball.

4 LOOSEN THE ROOTS IF NECESSARY. If the tree is overly root bound (with lots of roots circling the outer perimeter of the root ball since they didn't have anywhere else to go), you'll want to either loosen a great number of these roots or take your knife and make a few top-to-bottom slices across the sides of the root ball, freeing up the roots and encouraging them to grow outward.

5 **PLACE THE TREE IN THE HOLE.** This step is pretty easy, although you'll want to carefully survey the tree from all angles to ensure that the trunk is standing straight and true and not leaning. If necessary, add a little more dirt to the bottom of the hole to prop up the low side of the root ball.

STEP-BY-STEP

6 REFILL THE HOLE. With the root ball in place, you can now add dirt back into the hole to lock the tree in place. While you want to pack in the dirt securely, you don't need to go overboard in smashing It down as tightly as possible—that will just compact the soil and make it difficult for water and air to penetrate, eliminating any advantage gained from digging a wide hole to begin with.

STEP-BY-STEP

7 **WATER THOROUGHLY!** Trees grown in pots are accustomed to being watered regularly and abundantly at their nursery, and you'll need to do the same while they settle into their new environments. While the exact amount necessary will vary widely depending on the size of your tree and the conditions of the soil in your area, plan on watering your tree daily during the first two weeks after planting. After that, you can shift to once a week for the next year or so, after which the tree should be well established and ready to care for itself. Now, consider protecting it from deer and mice—details in another project (see page 78).

Protect a Fruit Tree

SKILL LEVEL:
Easy

TIME REQUIRED:
1 hour

Assuming that you have already completed the previous project (and who wouldn't want to plant a fruit tree?), you might want to consider going the extra mile and putting measures in place to protect your tree from wildlife such as deer, rabbits, mice, and voles.

Basically, this is a two-stage project involving the construction of a fence around the tree (to keep out large animals) and the installation of a plastic wrap around the trunk (to prevent small critters from chewing on the tree).

PARTS LIST

- 4 metal T-posts, 8 ft. (244 cm) tall
- 1 roll of welded wire, 8 ft. (244 cm) tall and at least 25 ft. (7.6 m) long
- 3 short pieces of string or wire
- Numerous zip ties
- Plastic tree wrap

TOOLS NEEDED

- Stake driver
- Ladder
- Tape measure
- Tape

Of course, within these broad parameters there are countless options for trunk wrap and the size and style of fencing. For example, do you stick with a tape-style wrap that winds up the trunk in overlapping fashion, or is it better to choose a thicker, solid piece of plastic that can be wrapped around the trunk to form a tube? Our personal preference is for the latter, since it can be easy to damage the bark of young trees if you leave tape-style wrap in place too long, and that's the method we'll cover here, although there are pros and cons to each option and you're free to use whatever makes sense for your own situation.

As for the style of fencing, since it's unlikely to be a permanent fixture (you're mainly looking to protect the tree while it's young), a simple welded wire fence held up by metal T-posts is both easy to construct and easy to take down when your tree is ready to survive on its own.

STEP-BY-STEP

1 **WRAP THE TREE TRUNK WITH PLASTIC.** The first step couldn't be much simpler. In the fall, wrap the trunk of your tree with a sheet of plastic tree wrap (make sure the side facing out is white), taking care to ensure that the bottom of the sheet is firmly pushed against the ground. Don't overtighten the sheet, but do keep it relatively snug against the trunk. Secure it in place using tape or string, then make a mental note to adjust its size every spring so that the tree can grow!

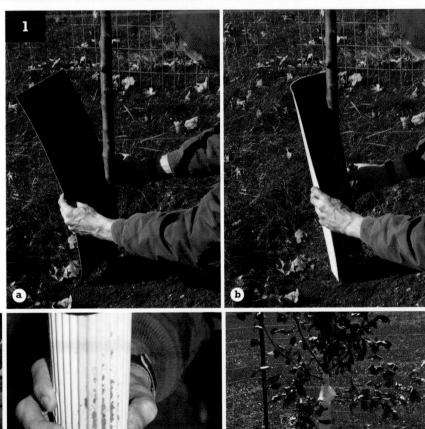

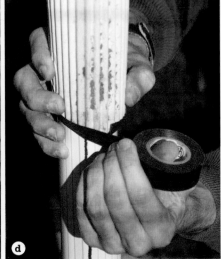

2

PLACE THE T-POSTS. Choose the locations for the four T-posts, which will mark the corners of your fence. Be sure to leave extra room around your tree so that the branches can grow outward for a year or two without bumping into the fence. At a minimum, make sure that the stakes are six feet (two meters) apart from each other. Install the T-posts using a stake driver (due to the height of the stakes, you might need to stand on a ladder—find a helper if you need one).

3 **INSTALL THE WIRE.** Measure the perimeter formed by the stakes to determine the amount of welded wire you will need, then add a foot or two to the result to give yourself some wiggle room (it can be difficult to pull welded wire so that it's tight around corners). Choose any stake and attach one end of the wire to it using large zip ties. Then continue around the perimeter (either direction), attaching wire to the remaining three stakes.

4

TIE OFF THE END OF THE WIRE. By now, the tree should be securely surrounded by wire on three sides, with one side still open. This side will serve as your "gate." Secure the loose end of your wire to the first stake using approximately three pieces of string or wire that can be easily removed at your convenience, thus opening up the gate. This way, you can still access the interior of the fence for weeding, pruning, and harvesting fruit.

STEP-BY-STEP

With these steps, you should be able to easily—and quickly—protect your young fruit trees from troublesome deer and smaller chewing critters like mice and voles. You'll thank yourself next year!

Build a Rabbit Nest Box

SKILL LEVEL:
Easy

TIME REQUIRED:
1 to 2 hours

Rabbits can make an excellent addition to many small hobby farms. For children—and adults, for that matter!—rabbits can serve as an easy-to-care-for introduction into livestock management. Rabbits are inexpensive to obtain and feed, easy to handle (as opposed to a larger species of livestock), and keeping them usually requires only minimal infrastructure. In fact, building your own rabbit housing and supplies is a project well within the capabilities of any experienced do-it-yourselfer. Hey! What a great idea—why not construct your own rabbit supplies yourself?

CUT LIST

- 1   7 × 7 in. (178 × 178 mm)   ½ in. (13 mm) plywood (top)
- 1   7 × 13 in. (178 × 330 mm)   ½ in. (13 mm) plywood (bottom)
- 2   8 × 14 in. (203 × 355 mm)   ½ in. (13 mm) plywood (sides)
- 1   5 × 7 in. (127 × 178 mm)   ½ in. (13 mm) plywood (front)
- 1   7 × 8 in. (178 × 203 mm)   ½ in. (13 mm) plywood (back)

PARTS LIST

- Box of 1 in. (25 mm) nails

TOOLS NEEDED

- Circular saw
- Hammer
- Tape measure
- Pencil

To get started, we can't think of a better option than to build a rabbit nest box. It serves as a great introductory rabbit-themed project. When raising rabbits, nest boxes are an important component of your necessary supplies. A nest box is an essential addition to the hutch of any pregnant doe, as her kits (baby rabbits) will use this box as their nursery for their first few weeks of life.

It can also be a fine idea to provide nest boxes for other rabbits as well, regardless of whether or not they are raising litters of kits. Most rabbits love having the option of a nice place to hide, and a nest box offers this protective place in the hutch. But there are other benefits to nest boxes as well. A nest box with a flat top (as we build in this project) provides rabbits with an elevated place to sit, which many rabbits seem to prefer, and most rabbits enjoy being able to hop up and down off of a nest box for extra entertainment.

But mainly, the primary goal of a nest box is to keep baby rabbits warm and grouped together in one place. Kits are born blind and hairless, and it's critical that they huddle together for warmth. If a nest box is too large, the kits may not stay together and thus won't stay as warm. The ideal dimensions of a nest box are determined by the size of the doe, and generally speaking a nest box should be just slightly larger than the size of the rabbit.

For this project, we'll construct an 8 × 14 × 8 in. (203 × 355 × 203 mm) nest box that is a suitable size for smaller breeds of rabbits, like Holland lops and others. For larger breeds, you'll want to modify these dimensions to construct a larger box, such as 9 × 15 × 9 in. (228 × 381 × 228 mm), or 11 × 16 × 11 in. (279 × 406 × 279 mm). According to the American Rabbit Breeders Association, "The nest box needs to be large enough to allow the doe to enter and turn around."

Keep in mind that warmth is the primary purpose of the nest box. Because of this, we prefer wooden nest boxes. Some pet supply stores offer stainless steel or wire nest boxes, and while these can be effective choices—perhaps in warm climates—it's simple to build wooden nest boxes using plywood or scrap lumber. The floor of the nest box can be made from solid plywood, or pegboard with holes. The pegboard holes allow for urine to escape and permit extra airflow (potentially helpful in warm climates), but it's possible for a baby rabbit's tiny foot to slip through the holes. For the safety and warmth of kits, we prefer a solid bottom board. Once your nest box is finished, just add a disposable cardboard liner (you'll replace this after each litter), some pine shavings, and some hay, then place it in your doe's hutch and wait for your new litter to arrive! If the nest box is for the enjoyment of a non-pregnant rabbit, you can skip the cardboard and shavings and just let the rabbit have fun with the box itself.

STEP-BY-STEP

1 **PREPARE AND MODIFY MATERIALS.** Constructing your wooden rabbit nest box requires only six small pieces of ½ in. (13 mm) plywood (refer to the cut list). Alternatively—because all of the pieces are small—you could utilize scrap lumber that isn't plywood, but plywood is nice because it is very strong and usually won't split even when you're nailing together narrow pieces.

Before construction begins, you'll need to make a simple modification to each of the 8 × 14 in. (203 × 355 mm) side pieces. It's just one diagonal cut: on the long side, measure and place a mark at 7½ in. (190 mm). Then on the short side, measure and place a mark at 5 in. (127 mm). Next draw a straight line between your two marks and cut off the small triangular piece with a circular saw. Easy! Repeat with the second 8 × 14 in. (203 × 355 mm) piece, and then discard the triangular pieces.

2 **ASSEMBLE THE NEST BOX, PART 1.** It might be beneficial to first "build" the nest box once without nails as a dry run, by simply holding each piece in place so you can visualize how they all fit together. To do this, simply take your newly-modified 8 × 14 in. (203 × 355 mm) sides and your 7 × 13 in. (178 × 330 mm) bottom piece and stand them up, positioning them into a "U" shape. The bottom should be centered, leaving ½ in. (13 mm) on each end. Next, add in the 7 × 8 in. (178 × 203 mm) back, 5 × 7 in. (127 × 178 mm) front, and 7 × 7 in. (178 × 178 mm) top. The front and back pieces sit "inside" the two sides, while the top piece literally sits on top of everything.

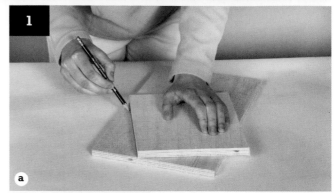

1

a

b

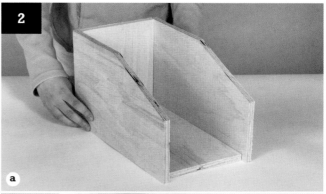

2

a

b

3 ASSEMBLE THE NEST BOX, PART 2.

Now you can actually construct the nest box, working each section at a time, as shown. You can use a hammer and nails as we did, or you could use an air nailer, or you could pre-drill holes with an electric drill. However you choose to assemble the nest box, you'll likely find that it's easier to tip the box on its side for nailing and continue to flip it around depending on where you're working. There's no right or wrong way to do this—whatever is comfortable and safe for you is the way to go.

The angled opening allows easy access for your doe to enter and exit the nest box, while the 5 in. (127 mm) front board keeps the babies safely enclosed in the box and prevents them from crawling out.

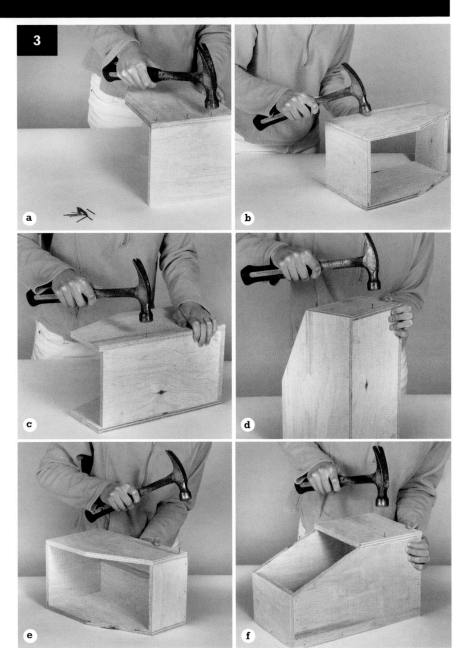

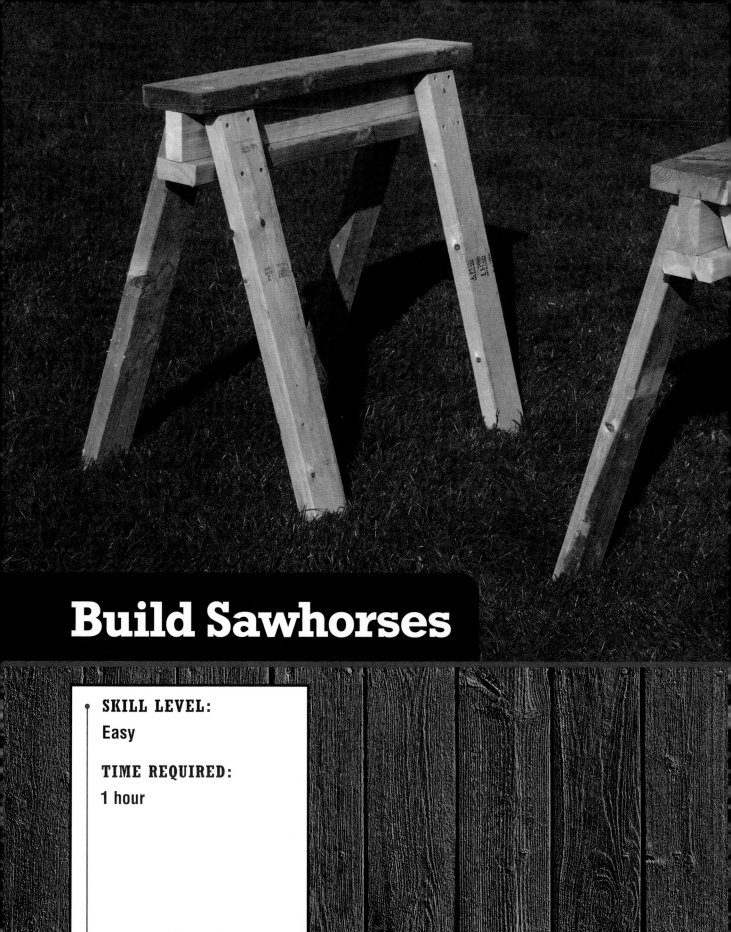

Build Sawhorses

SKILL LEVEL:
Easy

TIME REQUIRED:
1 hour

When you work on a farm, there is always some kind of repair task or construction job that needs your attention, and this often means you'll be doing some basic carpentry work. Whether you're building new stalls in the barn, repairing a machine shed roof, or building yourself an old-fashioned stone boat (see page 98), it's a necessity for a farmer to also have some woodworking knowledge and familiarity with the tools that go with it.

CUT LIST
- 12   31 in. (78.7 cm)   2×4s (6 for each sawhorse)
- 2   31 in. (78.7 cm)   2×6s (1 for each sawhorse)

PARTS LIST
- Box of 3 in. (76 mm) screws

TOOLS NEEDED
- Circular saw or miter saw (miter saw is useful for all the short 2×4 cuts)
- Tape measure
- Pencil
- Square
- Electric drill

That's why a set of basic sawhorses is an important tool for any working or hobby farm. Sawhorses are versatile: they're essential for safely and easily crosscutting lumber, they're great for staging sorted lumber prior to use, they save all kinds of wear on your back, and, in a pinch, you can throw a sheet of plywood or a couple of planks over the top of them and have an instant, portable work table. And this leads us to another point: you really need multiple sets of sawhorses. For a big project, one set just isn't enough!

You can purchase sawhorses, of course, but in the DIY spirit of this book, we're going to show you how to make your own sawhorses from scratch. The design here is simple and doesn't allow for folding, but the sawhorses are very strong.

The materials required are minimal, and the construction process itself is fast and well within the scope of an hour's work. Because of this, you can build yourself several sets (hint: think mass production and make all of the similar cuts for all your sawhorses at the same time) for less than you would spend for similarly-functioning products from a home-improvement center. Also, these sawhorses are stackable, so they won't take up as much space in your shop, barn, or garage.

You'll notice in the photos that the colors of the wood we used vary a little bit in shade; this is because we built these sawhorses entirely out of scrap material already leftover from other projects, including some 2×4s from a goat stall we renovated in our barn. The varying color doesn't matter a bit for the functionality of the sawhorses, and who isn't looking for ways to re-use things and save a little cash? The pieces of lumber required for this project are all fairly short, so this project is an ideal use for scrap lumber.

STEP-BY-STEP

1 **MAKE CUTS AND MEASUREMENTS.** For each individual sawhorse you build, you'll need a total of six 31 in. (78.7 cm) 2×4s, and a single 31 in. (78.7 cm) 2×6. Again, scrap lumber can be put to use, but if you do need to purchase 2×4s for this project, buying 8 ft. (2.4 m) lengths can work well. Eight feet is 96 inches (243 centimeters), so you'll get three 31 in. (78.7 cm) 2×4s out of each piece with very little waste.

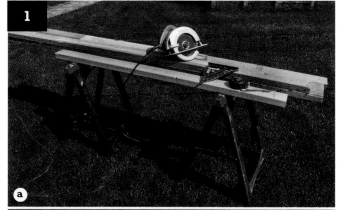

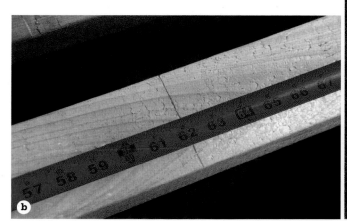

STEP-BY-STEP

2 BUILD THE I BEAM, PART 1. This style of sawhorse is built on an I beam frame. To begin with, take two of your 2×4s and screw them together to form a "T" shape, as shown. Center the "T" by making two marks set in at 1 and 2½ in. (25 and 63 mm). Secure firmly with 3 in. (76 mm) screws.

3 BUILD THE I BEAM, PART 2. Next, flip over your "T" and finish constructing the I beam by attaching the 2×6 to the top. This time, center it with marks at 2 and 3½ in. (51 and 89 mm). Using a 2×6 for the top of the sawhorses provides a broad and stable workspace, but if you prefer, you can swap out the 2×6 for just another 2×4. The choice is yours.

4 **ATTACH LEGS.** Now you can use your remaining 2×4s as legs for each corner. Set in the legs by 2 in. (51 mm) from the outside, and then use 3 in. (76 mm) screws to create a secure fit. Use four screws on each leg, two into the center of the I beam, and two into the lower part of it, as shown. When you're done, you'll have a very sturdy workplace for sawing and staging lumber. (And now you can use these sawhorses as you complete the rest of the projects in this book!)

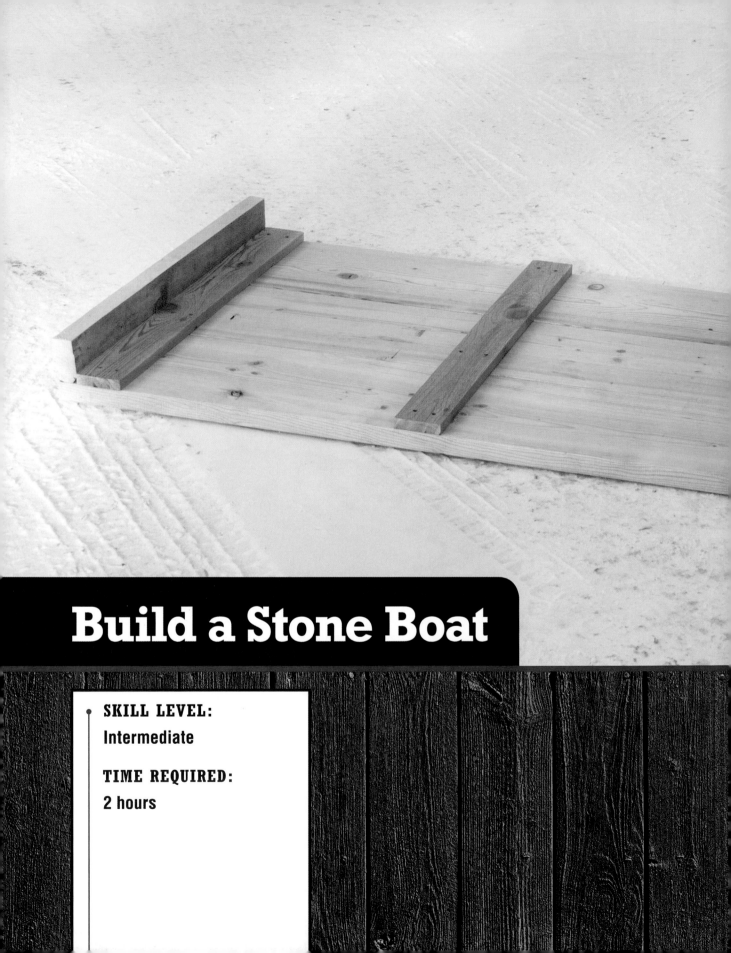

Build a Stone Boat

SKILL LEVEL:

Intermediate

TIME REQUIRED:

2 hours

If you've ever started a garden from scratch, or grown any type of crop on your farm, you've likely discovered something that countless other farmers have encountered in the centuries before you: too many rocks! Not only the many small, fist-sized stones that you find in your fields and garden soil, but also larger boulders that are heavy enough to leave you thinking: "how am I going to move that?"

CUT LIST

- 3   5 ft. (152 cm)   2×12s
- 1   33¾ in. (85.7 cm)   2×12
- 1   33¾ in. (85.7 cm)   2×4
- 3   33¾ in. (85.7 cm)   1×2s
- 2   15 × 11 in. (381 × 279 mm)
       approx. ½ or ¾ in.(13 or 19 mm) plywood

PARTS LIST

- Box of 1½ in. (38 mm) screws
- Box of 3½ in. (89 mm) screws

TOOLS NEEDED

- Circular saw
- Table saw (optional)
- Electric drill
- Jigsaw
- Square

For situations like these, we're often so quick to turn to modern machines and conveniences that we sometimes overlook other simple yet effective vintage techniques. Obviously, farmers have had to deal with stones for centuries, and if you need proof, just explore the property lines and field edges of older rural homesteads—you'll find literally miles of rock piles. So how did they move those rocks without modern machinery?

One simple way to move heavy loads is to make use of a *stone boat*. A stone boat—sometimes called a stone drag—is essentially a kind of low sled that can be used to move heavy loads like boulders, piles of rocks, large tree stumps, and other large items without having to actually lift them. Traditionally pulled by draft animals in the past, stone boats today work well with ATVs, UTVs, compact tractors, or garden tractors (some folks even continue to put their draft horses to work with this tool). Stone boats are appealing in their simplicity and usefulness; in many cases they are quick and easy to set up, load, transport, and dump. They may be old-fashioned, but they can be an actual timesaver today. In addition, they're interesting.

The instructions given here are for just one possible plan for a stone boat. The directions can easily be modified to your specific needs and wants by making the stone boat longer or wider. The flat "toboggan" style shown here is beneficial for moving large rocks and stumps, as these can be simply rolled onto the boat without any lifting required. This is nice because you can take your time and carefully roll large stones around until they are on the back of the stone boat. However, if you'd like the stone boat to carry loads of smaller rocks, simple low sides can be added. Some people prefer to add basic runners to the bottom of the stone boat for easier towing, but this raises the height of the bed, making it more difficult to roll large stones onto the deck.

Keep in mind that you can't back up a stone boat once it's loaded, so plan your route in advance before loading. Naturally, using the stone boat may cause some wear and tear on the surface of the ground, but in most cases the stone boat will be used in situations where this isn't a concern (uncleared fields, for example).

If you'd like a simple tool for moving heavy objects without having to lift them, then a stone boat is something you may want to build for your farm. We find them quite useful around our place.

STEP-BY-STEP

1 **MODIFY THE 2×12S FOR THE BASE.** The base of the stone boat is made up of three 5 ft. (152 cm) 2×12s laid out side by side. To help make the boat easier to drag, we'll start by modifying the "front" ends of these three 2×12s. Using a circular saw (or table saw), trim a 45° angle off the "short" ends, as shown.

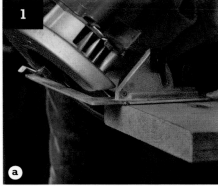
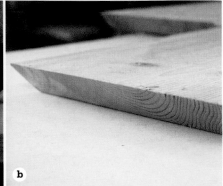

2 **MODIFY THE 2×12 FOR THE FRONT.** The single 33¾ in. (85.7 cm) 2×12 will be used on the front of the stone boat and help it to slide more easily, but it needs to be modified as well. Again, trim a 45° angle, but this time do it across the "long" end. Since this edge of the board will be rounded somewhat, it may help to draw a guideline set in at about ⅛ in. (3 mm) to help make the cut. Set this piece aside for the moment.

3 FASTEN THE BASE TOGETHER. Now, use the three 1×2s to join together the three 5 ft. (152 cm) 2×12s into a base for the stone boat. Place one of the 1×2s a distance of 1½ in. (38 mm) in from the back (non-trimmed) end of the stone boat. Place another 1×2 a distance of 3¾ in. (95 mm) in from the front (trimmed) end of the stone boat. Attach the third 1×2 in the center of the stone boat, at a distance of 21 in. (53 cm) from each of the other 1×2s. Use a square to help you get everything straight, and then use 1½ in. (38 mm) screws to fasten.

4 ADD THE "TAILGATE." For additional strength, and to help prevent loads from slipping off the back of the stone boat, add a simple 2×4 to the back of the stone boat; fasten this with 3½ in. (89 mm) screws (you might want to flip the stone boat over for this step, as we did).

STEP-BY-STEP

5 **ATTACH THE FRONT 2×12.** Add the single 33¾ in. (85.7 cm) 2×12 to the front of the stone boat, positioned as shown. Attach it with a combination of 1½ in. (38 mm) screws on the top and 3½ in. (89 mm) screws from underneath.

6 FASTEN PLYWOOD BRACES. To help add extra support to the angled front of the stone boat, a brace of some sort is desirable. This could be as simple as a set of 1×1s fastened between the top of the front board to the stone boat's base, or you can make the brace stronger (and better looking) by using two small sections of plywood. For our stone boat, we used two pieces of ¾ in. (19 mm) plywood, approximately 15 × 11 in. (381 × 279 mm), and then used a circular saw and jigsaw to refine the shape into something that would conform well with the shape of the stone boat. You can make the shape of the plywood less elaborate if you'd prefer. Either way, these braces add extra strength to the stone boat.

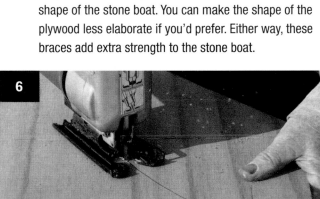

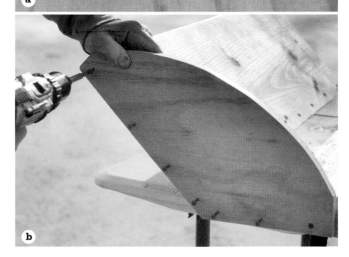

7 ADD A TOW OPTION. There are multiple ways you can tow your stone boat. Adding a pair of eye bolts can make the stone boat usable with a chain, or you can simply drill a pair of holes to add a tow rope, as we did here. Drill two holes, just large enough for the diameter of your chosen rope, through each of the plywood braces, then knot the ends of the rope to secure.

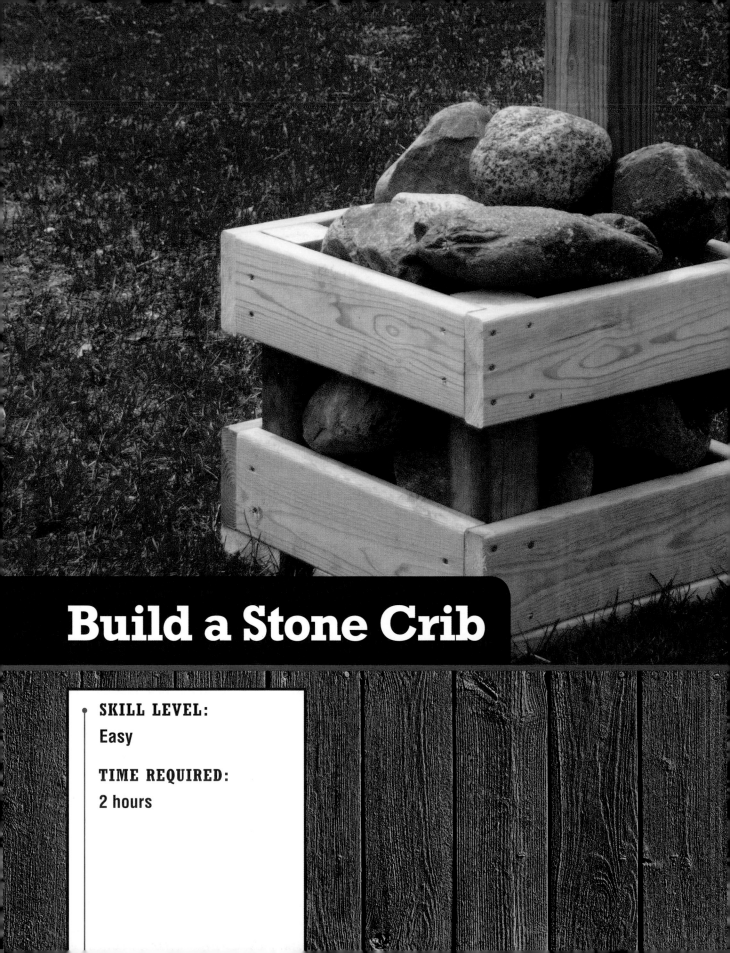

Build a Stone Crib

SKILL LEVEL:
Easy

TIME REQUIRED:
2 hours

Whether you fence your farm with wood, electric, or another type of fencing, traditional construction techniques usually require that you set your fence posts directly into the ground, perhaps with the aid of concrete as backfill. With corner posts in particular, achieving secure contact with the ground is critical, especially when using fencing under tension that exerts a constant pull on the corners.

CUT LIST
- 11   20 in. (51 cm)   2×6s
- 2   16½ in. (42 cm)   4×4s
- 1   6 ft. (182 cm) fence post (4×4, 4×6, 6×6—whatever you have handy)

PARTS LIST
- 4   3 in. (76 mm) angle brackets
- box 3 in. (76 mm) exterior screws
- box 4 in. (101 mm) exterior screws
- 1 pile of stones

TOOLS NEEDED
- Circular saw
- Chop/miter saw (optional)
- Electric drill
- Square
- Tape measure

Unfortunately, soil conditions are not always ideal in every spot where a post might be required. Farmers and ranchers often find themselves challenged by ground conditions that are too soft, muddy, sandy, or rocky to set a post in the traditional way. Cold regions face additional challenges, since it's not uncommon for deep spring frosts to repeatedly push fence posts upward from below, causing troublesome fencing dilemmas. A simple solution would be nice for these instances—so what can be done?

Enter the stone crib. A stone crib is essentially a wooden or wire cage or crate filled with rocks and used to secure a fence post without having to set the post directly into the soil. The stone crib simply rests on top of the ground, with the heavy load of stones holding the fence post in position.

The instructions here in this project are for an easy-to-build stone crib design that shouldn't take much time to construct and requires only a minimum of materials. The exact size of the crib you build (and therefore the number of rocks it will hold) will depend on your particular location and fencing needs. A corner post under tension—perhaps an electric fence—may require a larger number of rocks to hold it steady, while a simple line post (which we build here) can get away with fewer. Fortunately, it's a simple matter to adjust the measurements in this project to increase the dimensions of the stone crib; simply change the lengths of the eleven 2×6s from 20 in. (51 cm) to perhaps 24 in. (61 cm), or even 36 in. (91 cm) for a very large stone crib suitable for heavy-duty needs. Treated lumber will last longer.

These stone cribs are a wonderful little piece of rural ingenuity and a fine example of "using what you have"—in this case, using up those piles of rocks you've collected from plowing your fields and gardens.

1 **BUILD THE CRIB FRAMES.** Using 3 in. (76 mm) exterior screws, combine four of the 2×6s to create a rectangle. Use a framing square if necessary to keep the corners accurate. Repeat this step so that you have two identical frames.

STEP-BY-STEP

2

ADD FLOORBOARDS. Now add three additional 2×6s across one of the frames, leaving a gap of 3¼ in. (82 mm) inches as shown. This will be the bottom of the stone crib, but it is easier to build "upside down" and then flip it over. Use 3 in. (76 mm) screws to attach.

3

ATTACH THE CORNER 4×4S. For added strength, short 16½ in. (42 cm) 4×4s are used on two corners of the crib. Fasten these with 3 in. (76 mm) exterior screws on the sides and the bottom.

4

ATTACH THE SECOND FRAME. Using 3 in. (76 mm) screws, attach the second frame of 2×6s to the 4×4s. Leave a space of about 5½ in. (140 mm) between the two frames.

5 **FASTEN THE FENCE POST.** Now the stone crib is prepared to the point that you can actually attach the fence post it is designed to support. You can use whatever size fence post you have handy and that is large enough for the job; here we used a piece of 4×6 lumber. The post will need to be shorter than most fence posts you're used to working with because it won't be going in the ground; we cut ours to 6 ft. (182 cm). Use 4 in. (101 mm) screws to attach the post to the crib. Be especially careful when working with the project at this point, because until the rocks are added for weight, the stone crib will be top heavy and will easily tip over.

6 **ADD ANGLE BRACKETS.** For added strength, you can add four angle brackets to help hold the fence post to the stone crib as we did here.

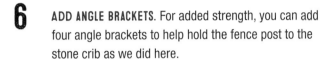

7 **FILL WITH STONES.** Move your empty stone crib into the location where you plan to use it, and then begin to fill the crib with stones. The weight of the rocks sitting in the crib provides a solid and stable foundation to hold the fence post, all without any digging or setting into the ground.

Build a Beehive

SKILL LEVEL:
Advanced

TIME REQUIRED:
About 8 hours, including
paint drying time

Modern beekeepers owe a great debt to Reverend Lorenzo Lorraine Langstroth (1810–1895)—inventor of what we today call the Langstroth hive. While the common dimensions used in hives today differ than what Langstroth patented in the 19th century, it's the concept—and its use of "bee space"—that sets this hive style apart.

PARTS LIST

- 1 17 × 23¼ in. (43.2 × 59 cm) flashing (aluminum or galvanized, optional for telescoping outer cover)
- Box of 1½ in. (38 mm) finish nails

TOOLS NEEDED

- Finish nailer
- Jigsaw
- Table saw
- Chop saw
- Circular saw
- Tape measure
- Rubber mallet
- Wood glue

CUT LIST

FOR THE HIVE BASE

- 2   22 in. (56 cm)   ¾ × 2 in. (19 × 51 mm)   long sides of the rim
- 1   12¼ in. (311 mm)   ¾ × 1¼ in. (19 × 32 mm)   one short side of the rim
- 1   12¼ in. (311 mm)   ¾ × 1½ in. (19 × 38 mm)

Used for the other short side of the rim, but note this one is 1½ in. (38 mm) tall, rather than 1¼ in. (32 mm) like the other.

- 1   12¼ × 20½ in. (311 × 521 mm)   ¾ in. (19 mm) plywood   bottom

FOR ENTRANCE REDUCER

- 1   12¼ in. (311 mm)   ¾ × ¾ in. (19 × 19 mm)

FOR HIVE BODY (PER BOX)

- 2   13¾ in. (34.9 cm)   ¾ × 6⅝ in. (19 × 168 mm)   two short sides of the hive body
- 2   19³⁄₁₆ in. (48.7 cm)   ¾ × 6⅝ in. (19 × 168 mm)   two long sides of the hive body
- 2   4 in. (101 mm)   ¾ × 1¼ in. (19 × 32 mm)   handles on either end of the box

FOR THE INNER COVER

- 2   19 in. (48.2 cm)   ¾ × 1⅛ in. (19 × 28 mm)   long sides of the rim
- 2   13¾ in. (34.9 cm)   ¾ × 1⅛ in. (19 × 28 mm)   short sides of the rim
- 1   12 × 18¼ in. (305 × 463 mm)   ¼ in. (6 mm) plywood   top

FOR THE TELESCOPING OUTER COVER

- 2   15½ in. (39.4 cm)   ¾ × 1¾ in. (19 × 44 mm)   short sides of the rim
- 2   20¼ in. (51.4 cm)   ¾ × 1¾ in. (19 × 44 mm)   long sides of the rim
- 1   15½ × 21¾ in. (39.4 × 55.2 cm)   ¼ in. (6 mm) plywood   top

Prior to Langstroth, beekeepers couldn't easily access all areas of the hive, and harvesting honey often meant the hive had to be destroyed. But in designing his hive, Langstroth took advantage of a fascinating truth about honey bees: they will not attempt to fill in gaps that are about ⅜ in. (9 mm) wide (gaps much smaller or much larger they will fill with propolis or comb respectively). This fact made it possible to control where the bees build honeycomb, and the result is the modern beehive design that we employ today.

In a Langstroth hive, the areas where the honeycomb is built—that is, the hexagonal structures that the honey bees construct out of beeswax and use to store honey and pollen and raise brood—is confined to thin, long *frames*, which, because of the design of the hive, are easily removable without causing damage to the honeycomb or any or part of the hive. This feature has tremendous advantages for beekeepers, as it allows for the simple and safe inspection of the hive, and an easy way to look for the queen and examine the health of the brood and colony on the whole. Finally, it allows honey to be harvested without ruining the hive.

Beehives are readily available from honey bee mail order supply companies, so it's possible to dive right into beekeeping without having to build anything at all. However, the skills required to build a basic Langstroth hive aren't very complex, and choosing to build your own hive not only provides you with the satisfaction of being directly involved with the creation of your bees' home, it also can help keep costs down. Here's why: beehives only require small pieces

of lumber. Often, the lengths involved can be made out of short cutoffs from other projects—scraps of wood that otherwise would be tossed in the trash pile. You might be able to find useable materials for a project like this in the scrap pile of your local lumberyard. As long as you ask for permission first, people are often happy to see their unwanted scraps salvaged and repurposed into other projects. By doing this, you might be able to reduce the cost of building a hive down to practically nothing. But even if you have to purchase all of the lumber new, the cost of building a new hive will still likely be quite low.

Pine is often used for beehives, as it's a softwood that won't weigh as much in the finished project (honey is heavy—you'll be glad later that the hive itself isn't adding to the weight!). Cypress is also popular in southern states. Even if you're using scrap lumber, take care to select wood that doesn't have large knots that might cause cracking.

Hive boxes designed to hold ten frames are common, but more and more beekeepers are turning to the smaller eight-frame variety, which is what we illustrate here.

Some beekeepers use hive boxes of different depths for the upper and lower areas of the hive. Oftentimes the lower boxes—the "brood" boxes—are deeper at 9⅝ in. (244 mm), while the upper boxes—the "supers"— are shallower at 6⅝ in. (168 mm). Others forego the use of deep hive boxes and use 6⅝ in. (168 mm) supers for the entire hive, so it's possible that these instructions could be utilized to build an entire multi-box hive. The choice of using deep hive boxes or not is up to the individual beekeeper.

One thing we don't include here are instructions for building the actual hive frames, as you'll find it more practical to purchase these rather than build them from scratch, especially if you use frames with premade foundations, as many beekeepers do; still, building the hive boxes themselves represents a substantial savings. For hive boxes in the dimensions given here, you'll need eight frames for each box.

Building the beehive is a task that requires a bit of woodworking finesse, including some rabbet and dado cuts, but the DIYer with some good carpentry skills should find this a challenging and satisfying project to construct.

1

CONSTRUCT THE HIVE BASE. The base of the beehive is probably the most complicated, but even this step isn't very difficult. Naturally, the two 22 in. (56 cm) long sides of the rim will be positioned on the long sides of the 12¼ × 20½ in. (311 × 521 mm) plywood. The 1½ in. (38 mm) "tall" 12¼ in. (311 mm) rim piece will go on one short end of the plywood, and the other (we'll say "shorter") 1¼ in. (32 mm) 12¼ in. (311 mm) rim piece will go on the other end. It's the positioning of all this that is slightly tricky. In the photos you can see the goal: the piece nearest the camera is the "shorter" rim piece, and should be flush with the *bottoms* of the 22 in. (56 cm) rim pieces. On the opposite end of the hive base, the "taller" rim piece is flush with the *tops* of the 22 in. (56 cm) rim pieces. The plywood interior should be flush with the top of the front 1¼ in. (32 mm) short end rim piece; this will place the plywood ¾ in. (19 mm) down from the tops of the 22 in. (56 cm) boards. Whew! Sounds complicated, but it's really not that difficult. Use wood glue and nails to secure. The entrance reducer is shown here near its final location for illustration purposes.

1

STEP-BY-STEP

2

CONSTRUCT THE HIVE BODY. The hive body is fairly straightforward, depending on how you'd like to fasten the corners. You might see professionally manufactured hive bodies available from bee catalogs that feature dovetailed joint corners. While dovetailed joints are definitely strong, they can be complicated to construct, so for this project we recommend the simpler rabbet joint for the corners; basically a two-sided groove to provide extra strength on the joints and also to create a resting place for the bee frames.

To start, saw a ¾ × ⅜ in. (6 × 9 mm) rabbet within each end of both 13¾ in. (34.9 cm) short end pieces. Also saw a ⅝ × ⅜ in. (16 × 9 mm) rabbet along the tops of both 13¾ in. (34.9 cm) short pieces. This is the area where the frames will sit in the finished beehive.

Using wood glue and nails, fasten both short 13¾ in. (34.9 cm) pieces to the two longer 19³⁄₁₆ in. (48.7 cm) pieces to create the complete hive body.

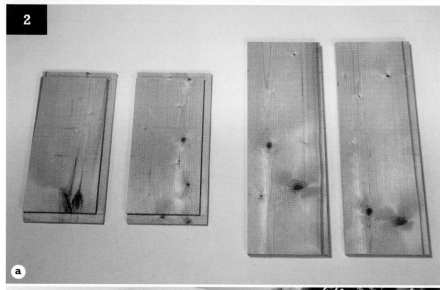

a

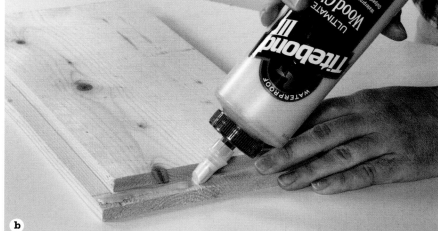

b

c

To make handles (you'll want them—a hive body full of honey is very heavy), bevel the top edges of the two 4 in. (101 mm) long ¾ × 1¼ in. (19 × 32 mm) pieces at 15°. Glue and nail these handles to the centers of the hive body's short sides.

Repeat step 2 again if you'd like to construct more than one hive body box (a good idea—you might want to make three or four to begin with).

d

e

f

g

3 **CONSTRUCT THE INNER COVER.** The inner cover consists of a 12 × 18¼ in. (305 × 463 mm) piece of ¼ in. (6 mm) plywood, surrounded by four rim pieces. We suggest centering a ¼ × ⅜ in. (6 × 9 mm) dado (a three-sided groove, not unlike a rabbet) into the edges of both 19 in. (48.2 cm) rim pieces and both 13¾ in. (34.9 cm) rim pieces. Additionally, saw ⅝ × 1⅛ (16 × 28 mm) from the corners of both 13¾ in. (34.9 cm) pieces as shown.

It's handy to have a handle for the inner cover, so use a jigsaw to create a 1 × 3½ in. (25 × 89 mm) oval hole in the center of the plywood. Using glue to fasten, slide the grooves of each slide rim piece onto the edges of the plywood. Then use glue and nails to fasten the corners to each other.

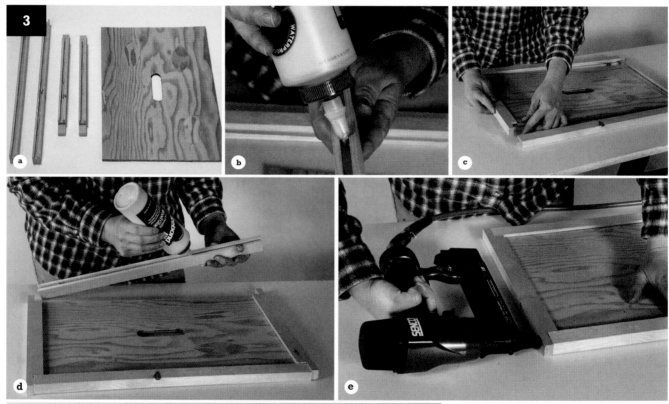

4

CONSTRUCT THE TELESCOPING OUTER COVER. Using the two longer 20¼ in. (51.4 cm) rim pieces and the two 15½ in. (39.4 cm) rim pieces, create a rectangle frame, with the longer pieces "inside" the shorter ones. Use glue and nails to fasten, and then nail the 15½ × 21¾ in. (39.4 × 55.2 cm) piece of ¼ in. (6 mm) plywood on top (how easy was that?). As protection against the weather, you can also add your 17 × 23¼ in. (43.2 × 59 cm) flashing at this stage. Use a rubber mallet to bend over the edges, and use nails to attach.

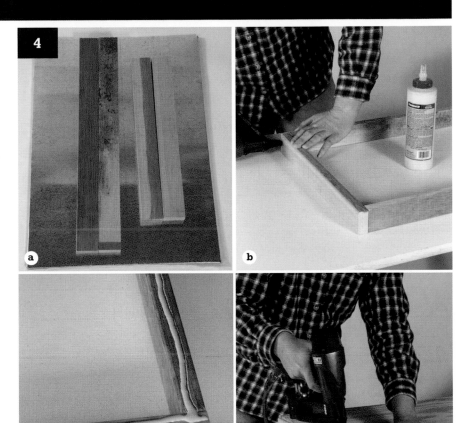

STEP-BY-STEP

5 **CONSTRUCT THE ENTRANCE REDUCER.** Preparing the hive's entrance reducer is a fairly simple matter. You'll need two notches:

- A notch 4½ × ⅜ in. (114 × 9 mm) located on the left half of the entrance reducer
- A second notch ¾ × ⅜ in. (19 × 9 mm) on the right half. For this, you'll need to rotate the entrance reducer 90°.

  The entrance reducer isn't actually fastened to the hive, it remains free and can be turned one way or the other to allow for a larger opening for the bees to use in summer and a smaller hole for winter (or for a weak colony).

6 **PAINT.** Your hive will need some paint to protect the wood and to make it look great. Paint the exterior edges with primer and finish coats or with a white stain. This step is pretty simple—and can be fun especially if you have extra help.

7

ADD FRAMES AND USE! Finally install your frames and put the hive to use! "Installing" a colony of bees into a new hive is an interesting and exciting job—but that's a topic for another book.

7

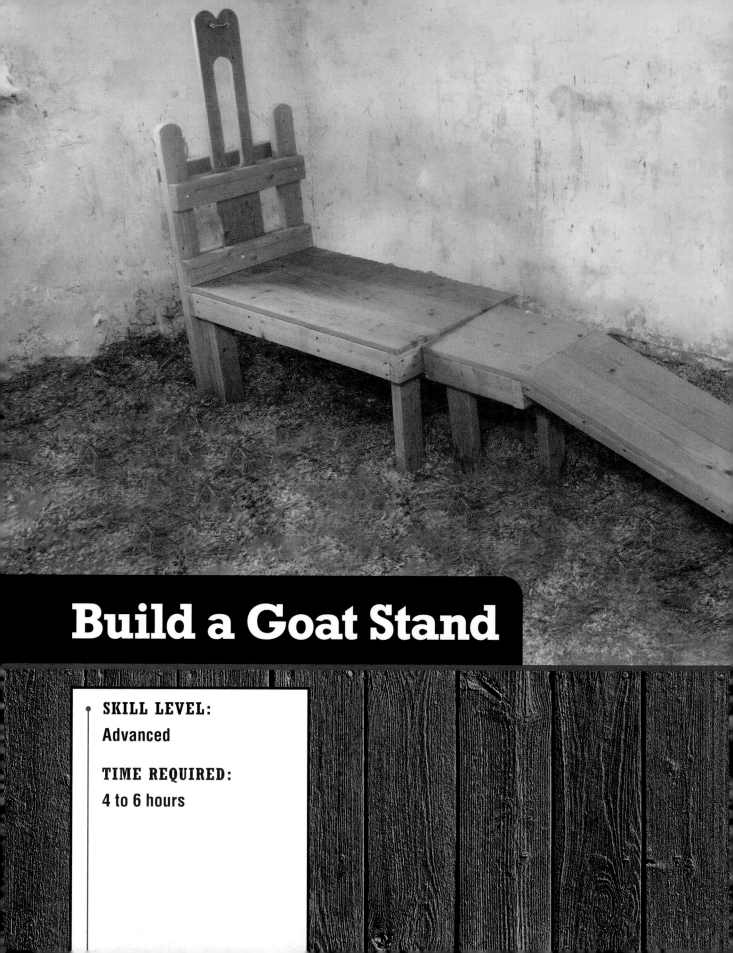

Build a Goat Stand

Although this type of stand is commonly known as a "milking stand," they're just as useful for meat goats as dairy goats. Whether you're grooming, trimming hooves, vaccinating, or administering medical care, you will definitely want this stand handy!

The headpiece frees you to work on whatever task needs doing, instead of struggling to hold your goat steady, and makes a one-person job out of chores that might have required two people before. Just put a little food in the feed pan, secure your goat's head, and get to work! The wide platform keeps your goat from stepping off and allows you to sit beside your goat if necessary.

This particular stand was designed for our Nigerian dwarf goats. If you have a standard-sized breed like an alpine or a Toggenburg, you'll need to adjust the size accordingly—particularly the height of the headpiece!—but the same basic design will work for any size goat.

TOOLS NEEDED

- Circular saw
- Jigsaw
- Radial arm saw
- Electric drill
- Finish nailer or hammer
- Wood clamps
- Tape measure
- Pencil
- Framing square
- Triangle square

PARTS LIST

- Box of 3 in. (76 mm) screws
- Box of 1½ in. (38 mm) screws
- Box of 1½ in. (38 mm) finish nails

CUT LIST

FOR THE MILKING STAND

- 4   17⅜ in. (44.1 cm)   2×4s (legs)

FOR THE FRAME RECTANGLE

- 2   36⅞ in. (93.6 cm)   2×4s (long sides)
- 2   22¼ in. (56.5 cm)   2×4s (short sides)
- 2   19¼ in. (48.9 cm)   2×4s (underneath brace separation 11¼ in. [286 mm])
- 3   40 in. (101 cm)   1×8s (surface planks)
- 2   13¾ in. (34.9 cm)   2×2s (spacers)

FOR THE STANCHION

- 2   40 in. (101 cm)   2×4s (rounded, big legs)
- 2   22⅜ in. (56.8 cm)   2×4s (front braces, no notches)
- 2   22⅜ in. (56.8 cm)   2×4s (back braces with notches)
- 1   22⅜ in. (56.8 cm)   2×6 (wing nuts)

FOR THE HEAD GATE

- 1   40 in. (101 cm)   1×8 (cut in half and modified top and bottom)
- 2   5½ in. (140 mm) wing nuts
- 1   6 in. (152 mm) bolt for swinging head gate
- 1   hook and eye

FOR THE RAMP

FOR THE SQUARE SEAT

- 2   14¾ in. (37.4 cm)   2×4s
- 2   11¾ in. (298 mm)   2×4s
- 3   17¼ in. (43.8 cm)   2×4s (legs)
- 1   10¼ in. (260 mm)   2×4

FOR THE SEAT SURFACE

- 2   14⅞ in. (37.8 cm)   1×8s

FOR THE RAMP UNDER FRAME

- 2   54½ in. (138 cm)   2×2s (long sides)
- 5   11¾ in. (298 mm)   2×2s (braces) (underneath brace separation 10¾ in. [273 mm])

FOR THE RAMP SURFACE

- 2   54⅝ in. (139 cm)   1×8s (with ¼ in. [6 mm] gap)

STEP-BY-STEP

The Stand

1 **ASSEMBLE THE STAND PLATFORM FRAME.** It's not too challenging to get started on this one, although some of the later steps are a bit more complex. To begin, build the basic rectangle frame of the milking stand's platform. To do this, use two 36⅞ in. (93.6 cm) 2×4s for the long sides, with two 22¼ in. (56.5 cm) 2×4s as the short sides. Position the 22¼ in. (56.5 cm) 2×4s so that they are on the "outside" of the longer sides, as shown. Also, attach two additional 2×4 braces to the interior, both 19¼ in. (48.9 cm) long. The separation between the braces should be about 11¼ in. (286 mm). Fasten with 3 in. (76 mm) screws.

2 **ADD THE FLOOR.** The "floor" of the milking stand consists of three 40 in. (101 cm) 1×8s, each separated by about ¼ in. (6 mm). These line up side by lengthwise across the frame, and are fastened with finish nails.

STEP-BY-STEP

3   **ADD THE LEGS.** It's a simple matter to attach the four legs of the milking stand, which are made from four 17⅜ in. (44.1 cm) 2×4s, and positioned as shown. Use 3 in. (76 mm) screws to fasten.

4   **ADD THE TALLER LEGS.** Another pair of taller legs—40 in. (101 cm)— are attached to the front of the milking stand, and fastened with 3 in. (76 mm) screws. Also two 13¾ in. (34.9 cm) 2×2 spacers are used to fill in the gap between the longer and shorter front legs. Additionally, rounding the tops of these 40 in. (101 cm) legs will make the goat stand look nicer.

5

ADD THE HEAD GATE. The head gate is made out of one modified 40 in. (101 cm) 1×8. First, rip the 1×8 in half down the middle, then use a jigsaw to form the neck opening, as shown. Also, modify a notch at the bottom of one of the head gates so that it will be able to open and close. This head gate needs to be able to move side to side, so a small hole and a 6 in. (152 mm) bolt and wing nut are used. The other head gate can be fastened with wood glue and 1½ in. (38 mm) screws. The tops of the head gates should be rounded as well, and a hook-and-eye added to the top.

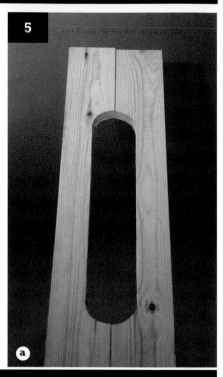

6   **ADD HEAD GATE BRACES.** Two sets of 22⅜ in. (56.8 cm) 2×4s are used on each side of the head gate to support it. Two of these 2×4s are unmodified, but the other two need be to notched in order to fit snugly around the head gate. A radial arm saw is ideal here for making these cuts. An additional 22⅜ in. (56.8 cm) 2×6 is used to hang a feeder to keep the goats happy while they're in the stand. Note also that we eventually drilled pairs of holes at varying heights into the 40 in. (101 cm) tall legs, and also through the 2×6 and upper pairs of 2×4s to allow the milking stand to be adjustable to variously sized goats. The 5½ in. (140 mm) bolts and wing nuts hold these together.

The Ramp

7 **BUILD THE SEAT.** The ramp for the milking stand is fairly simple to construct, and not only serves as a way for goats to climb up to the milking stand, but the flat end of the ramp can also double as a seat to use when milking. To start, use two 14¾ in. (37.4 cm) 2×4s and two 11¾ in. (298 mm) 2×4s to make a simple square frame. Three 17¼ in. (43.8 cm) 2×4 legs are used next, with two legs in opposite corners and another leg centered across from them as shown. A simple 10¼ in. (260 mm) 2×4 is used as an underneath brace. Finally, two 14⅞ in. (37.8 cm) 1×8s are put to use as the seat's surface, separated slightly.

8 **BUILD THE RAMP.** The frame of the ramp section comprises two 54½ in. (138 cm) 2×2s parallel to each other, and fastened together with five 11¾ in. (298 mm) 2×2s spaced about 10¾ in. (273 mm) apart. Also, two 54⅝ in. (139 cm) 1×8s are used as the ramp's surface, with a slight separation between them.

9 **MODIFY THE ANGLES.** Before attaching the ramp to the seat with 3 in. (76 mm) screws, you'll want to make slight adjustments to the angles at the bottom of the ramp and to the top where it fastens to the seat. Cut a shallow angle on the bottom of the ramp where it will rest on the floor, and another at the top of the ramp so that it lines up properly with the seat. Once finished, slowly introduce your goats to the new process of climbing up the ramp and onto the milking stand.

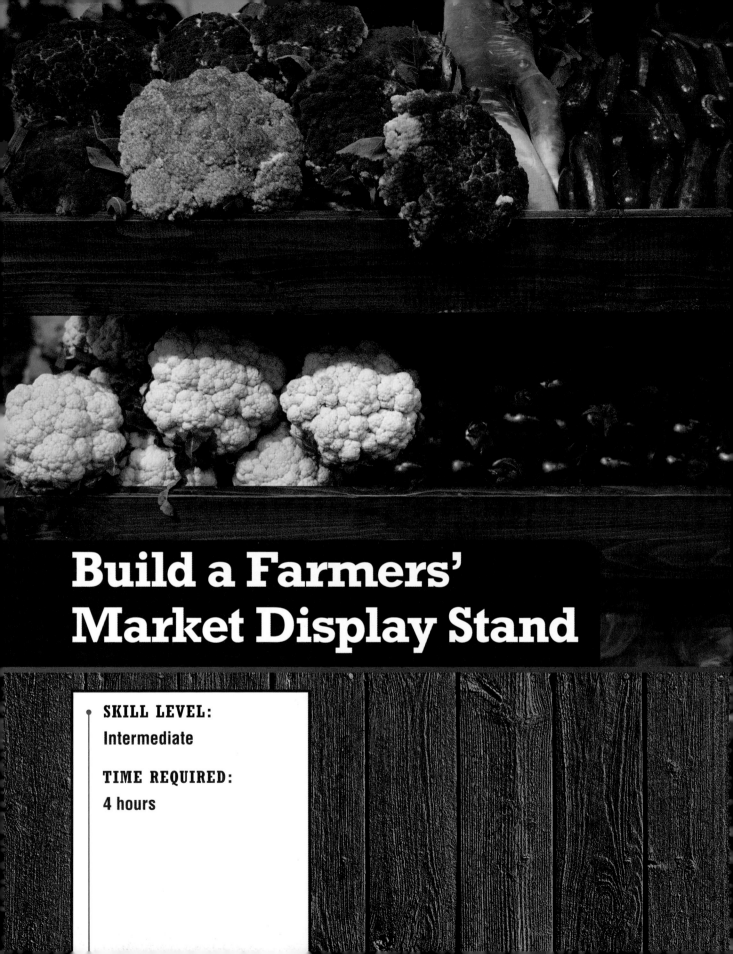

Build a Farmers' Market Display Stand

SKILL LEVEL:
Intermediate

TIME REQUIRED:
4 hours

You probably go to a lot of effort to plant, tend, and harvest your farm's apples, potatoes, squash, corn, and other produce. And you might go to even further effort bringing all of those crops to sell at the farmers' market. So after all your hard work, it's only fitting that your produce should have a nice spot to be displayed to the public, and that's what this project is all about. Our goal here is to build a fairly simple yet useful farmers' market stand with three large storage drawers that are slightly tilted to help display their contents. The whole unit is self-contained, large enough to hold plenty of produce (plus you can always build more than one of these if you need to), and it also includes a spot for an advertising sign.

Besides being fun to attend, farmers' markets can be an excellent way for small-scale and hobby farmers to distribute any excess fruits and vegetables that their gardens produce; for some, it can be a way for the farm to help pay you back for all the efforts you put into it.

TOOLS NEEDED

- Circular saw (miter saw can be helpful but not required)
- Tape measure
- Pencil
- Framing square
- Finish nailer
- Electric drill
- Jigsaw
- Level
- Sandpaper

CUT LIST

• 18	3 ft. (91 cm)	2×6s
• 6	20½ in. (52.1 cm)	2×6s
• 2	4 ft. (122 cm)	2×4s
• 2	5½ ft. (168 cm)	2×4s
• 2	3 ft. (91 cm)	2×4s

PARTS LIST

- 1   23 × 17 in. (58.4 × 43.2 cm) chalkboard
- Box of 3 in. (76 mm) screws
- Box of 1¾ in. (44 mm) screws
- Box of 1½ in. (38 mm) finish nails

STEP-BY-STEP

1 **MAKE CUTS AND SAND EDGES.** This project requires making quite a few cuts—especially all of the 1×6s—and this will take some time, but once everything is prepared, the construction process moves rather quickly. After making all of the necessary cuts, take a few moments to smooth off any rough edges on the 1×6s with sandpaper for a clean, finished look.

2 **ASSEMBLE THE DRAWERS, PART 1.** The drawers used to hold all of your wonderful farm and garden produce are going to be 3 ft. × 22 in. (91 × 55.9 cm) when completed. The main frame of each drawer is constructed from two 3 ft. (91 cm) 1×6s and two 20½ in. (52.1 cm) 2×6s. To ensure that the drawer's dimensions come out correctly, it's essential to place the shorter 20½ in. (52.1 cm) 1×6s on the *insides* of the longer 3 ft. (91 cm) 1×6s. Use a framing square to keep the angles right at 90°, and then use a finish nailer with 1½ in. (38 mm) nails to fasten each corner together. Take care to ensure that the corners are all flush with each other on every side before nailing.

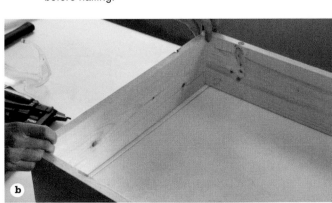

STEP-BY-STEP

3 ASSEMBLE THE DRAWERS, PART 2. Now take four additional 3 ft. (91 cm) 1×6s and use them to create the floor of the drawer (you're building the drawers upside down at this point). Again, get everything flush first and then fasten with 1½ in. (38 mm) nails. The combined width of the four 1×6s totals 22 in. (55.9 cm); this is why it's necessary for the 20½ in. (52.1 cm) sides of the drawers to go on the inside. The 20½ in. (52.1 cm) combined with the thickness of the long sides of the drawer equals 22 in. (55.9 cm)—just right for the four bottom boards. Repeat steps 2 and 3 two more times so that you have three complete, identical drawers.

EACH DRAWER:
- 3 ft. (91 cm)   front
- 3 ft. (91 cm)   back
- 20½ in. (52.1 cm)   side
- 20½ in. (52.1 cm)   side
- 3 ft. (91 cm)   bottom × 3

4

ROUND THE EDGES OF THE 2×4S. The legs of the farmers' market stand are simple 2×4s, 4 ft. (122 cm) tall in the front and 5½ ft. (168 cm) tall in the back. To improve the appearance of the stand and make it a little nicer, it's a good idea to round off the top edges of the legs. To do this, use a pencil to make a curved guideline; we used the lid from a coffee can as a stencil to help get the curve right. Then use a jigsaw to make the rounded cut. Finally, use sandpaper to smooth it out the rest of the way.

5

PREPARE THE DRAWERS FOR STAND CONSTRUCTION. Building the drawers requires care and attention to detail, but shouldn't be particularly tricky. This next part however, is a little more challenging, so take your time and perhaps get some help from a friend as you work.

To construct the stand correctly, the three drawers need to be square to each other, and also the same distance apart. To help get them square, lay out a long spare 2×4 on a flat surface like a garage or shop floor. With the three drawers standing upright on their sides, gently line up each drawer against the 2×4; this will help get them roughly square initially. Then use your tape measure to separate each drawer by 12 in. (305 mm). It may take some double-checking of all the distances a few times to get everything set correctly.

13

STEP-BY-STEP

6   **ADD LEGS.** Now you can gently set the legs in place. To create drawers that slant at the proper angle, it's important to make two precise measurements on each side:

- There should be 2½ in. (63 mm) between the bottom of the front leg and the bottom corner of the lower drawer.
- There should be 3½ in. (89 mm) between the top corner of the upper drawer and the edge of the front leg.

   For the back legs, use a framing square to make them square to the front legs; the back of the top drawer should sit flush with the edge of the back leg.

(a)

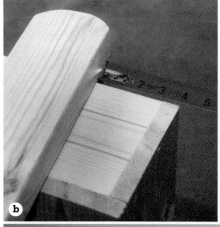

(b)

(c)

(d)

(e)

(f)

7

ADD A MOUNT FOR THE SIGN. We've purposely left the back legs of the farmers' market stand rather tall so that there is room to put up a sign or chalkboard to advertise your produce. To make a place to hang the sign, screw two 3 ft. (91 cm) 2×4s in between the two back legs, then nail or screw your sign or chalkboard into place. We used a chalkboard so that the advertising could be erased and reused as needed. Finally, you can stain the wood if you'd like.

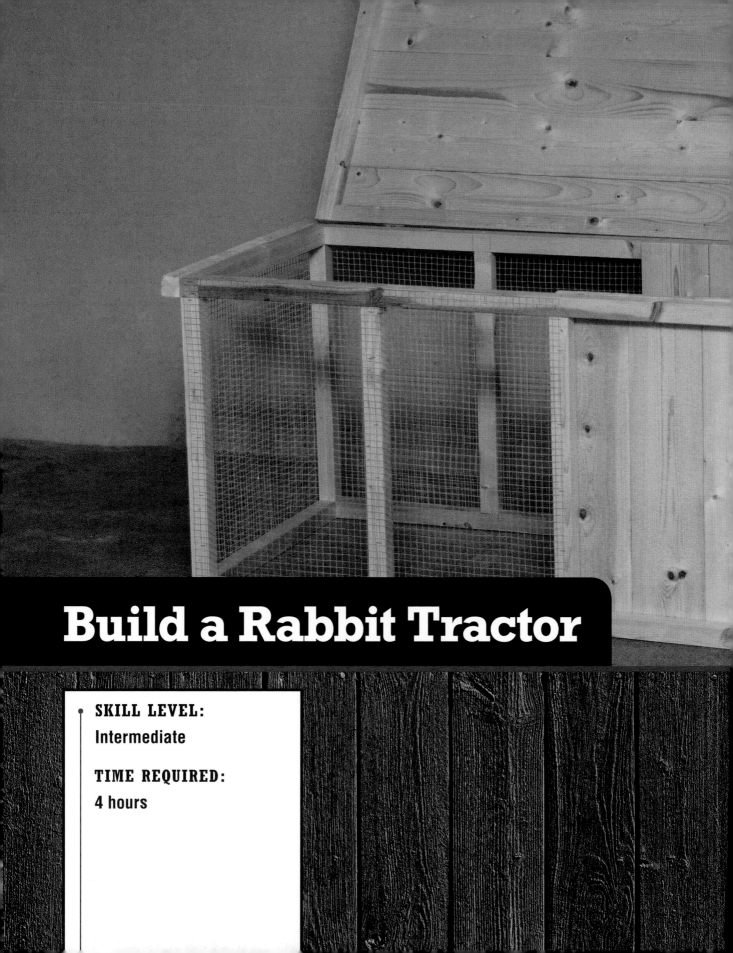

Build a Rabbit Tractor

SKILL LEVEL:
Intermediate

TIME REQUIRED:
4 hours

Raising rabbits is a fine way to get started with livestock farming. There are a number of good reasons for this: rabbits are relatively easy to care for, they're inexpensive, and they mature quickly. Some breeds are useful as meat animals, and all rabbits provide excellent fertilizer for gardens. For all of these reasons, farmers of all skill levels often enjoy keeping rabbits, and you can try it, too.

CUT LIST

- 6   45 in. (114 cm)   2×2s
- 8   25 in. (63.5 cm)   2×2s
- 8   22 in. (55.9 cm)   2×2s
- 10   25 in. (63.5 cm)   1×6s
- 5   4 ft. (122 cm)   1×6s

PARTS LIST

- 2   30 × 24½ in. (76 × 62.2 cm) sections of ½ in. (13 mm) hardware cloth
- 1   2 × 2 ft. (60.7 × 60.7 cm) section of ½ in. (13 mm) hardware cloth
- 2   2 in. (51 mm) hinges
- 1 hook and eye latch
- Box of 3 in. (76 mm) screws

TOOLS NEEDED

- Circular saw/miter saw
- Electric drill
- Finish nailer (optional)
- Hammer
- Staple gun
- Wire snips
- Tape measure
- Pencil
- Wood glue (optional)

Proper shelter for your rabbits is critical; they need a comfortable place to live that protects them from the weather and predators, and a quality rabbit hutch is often a popular choice for this. But even a good hutch doesn't always fully address the issue of a rabbit's exercise needs or provide them with a way to enjoy the outdoors. However, rabbits can't be "turned out" at pasture like larger livestock, as they will be at great risk from predators and exposure and you'd be unlikely to ever catch them again! One way to get around these issues is to provide your rabbits with a portable, contained exercise/grazing area that allows them to move around while still providing protection.

Enter the rabbit tractor. If you're at all familiar with a chicken tractor, you'll find this to be essentially the same concept. It aims to provide your rabbits with a "best of both worlds" scenario where they are able to get out during the day, enjoy some fresh air, munch on some fresh grass, and get some exercise, all while still being contained within a shady enclosure and protected from predators. The small size of the rabbit tractor has two benefits over a fixed fence: it's inexpensive to build, and easy to move, so you can move it around your property and prevent your rabbits from exhausting a particular area. It's vital that you keep your rabbit tractor away from any type of lawn surface that has been treated with pesticides, fertilizers, or the like. Also, avoid placing the tractor on any mowed surface with recent clippings still on the ground.

As convenient as a rabbit tractor is, it's not as secure as a hutch, and your rabbits should not be left in it unattended. The rabbit tractor requires a fairly level surface to rest on; too much of a slope or uneven ground may cause gaps to appear between the ground and the base of the tractor, which clever rabbits (or even not-so-clever rabbits!) may squeeze out of. Even on level ground, rabbits love to dig, and if you have a prolific digger, he may just be able to tunnel out from under the rabbit tractor (if this seems to be an issue with your rabbits, you can also consider fastening a sheet of ½ in. (13 mm) hardware cloth to the bottom of the rabbit tractor—this should keep the bunnies from digging but still allow them to nibble on grass). But there are more reasons to keep an eye on the rabbits while they are using the tractor. For one, you can watch for predators, but you can also monitor the comfort level of your rabbits: you'll be able to tell when they've had enough fun, or are getting too hot and are ready to retire to the comfort of their regular hutch. Don't expect your rabbits to use the rabbit tractor all day long—aim for short periods. Rabbits are sensitive to dietary changes, so you'll want to slowly build up the time they spend outside in order to prevent them from overindulging on grass before their digestive system has had time to adjust.

What we show here is just one possible design for the basic concept of the rabbit tractor. You could easily make yours longer or wider if you'd like to provide more room. For safety's sake, it's probably wisest to only allow one rabbit in the tractor at a time. Rabbits should always have a shady spot available to them, so we've included a solid roof, as well as a rear area with sides for additional shade in case the rabbits need it. The entire rabbit tractor roof is designed to open in one piece to aid in catching your rabbits (some may not easily cooperate!).

STEP-BY-STEP

1 **PREPARE THE LUMBER.** This project is fairly simple in that it only requires two types of lumber: 2×2s (also known as "furring strips") for the main frame, and 1×6s for the shade walls and roof. A miter saw will make quick work of the these cuts, but you can also use a circular saw.

a

b

c

2

BUILD THE SHORT END FRAMES. We'll start off by constructing two simple 25 × 25 in. (63.5 × 63.5 cm) square frames that will become the two short ends of the rabbit tractor. To do this, place two of the 25 in. (63.5 cm) 2×2s parallel to each other, and then insert two of the 22 in. (55.9 cm) 2×2s on the "insides" to create a precise 25 × 25 in. (63.5 × 63.5 cm) square, as shown. On this step (and the further framing steps), you can use a framing square before screwing to help you achieve exact 90° angles; this will help ensure that your rabbit tractor sits flush on the ground without wobbling. Use 3 in. (76 mm) screws to fasten the corners.

3

ADD THE LONG ENDS. Next use four of the 45 in. (114 cm) 2×2s to join your two square ends and create a rectangular box frame. The two 25 in. (63.5 cm) squares sit on the far outsides of the rabbit tractor, and the four 45 in. (114 cm) 2×2s are used simply to hold the structure together. Again, use 3 in. (76 mm) screws for construction and check your corners with the framing square as necessary.

4 **BUILD THE ROOF FRAME.** To start the roof of the rabbit tractor, simply build a basic rectangle out of the other two 45 in. (114 cm) 2×2s and two 25 in. (63.5 cm) 2×2s. The 25 in. (63.5 cm) 2×2s should go on the "outside." Fasten with 3 in. (76 mm) screws. When completed, this roof frame will match exactly the footprint of the main rabbit tractor frame.

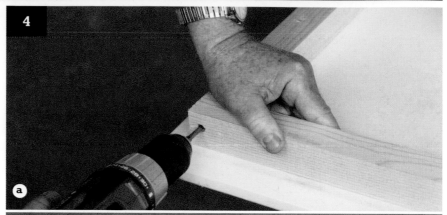

5

ATTACH SIDE BRACES. To help hold the hardware cloth in place and to provide "trim" for the shaded portion of the rabbit tractor, four additional 22 in. (55.9 cm) 2×2s are used as vertical side braces on the main tractor frame. Measuring from the inside of the rabbit tractor frame (on the 45 in. [114 cm] 2×2s), these side braces are centered on 13⅞ in. (35.2 cm) and 27¾ in. (70.5 cm) on each side. The photos help illustrate this.

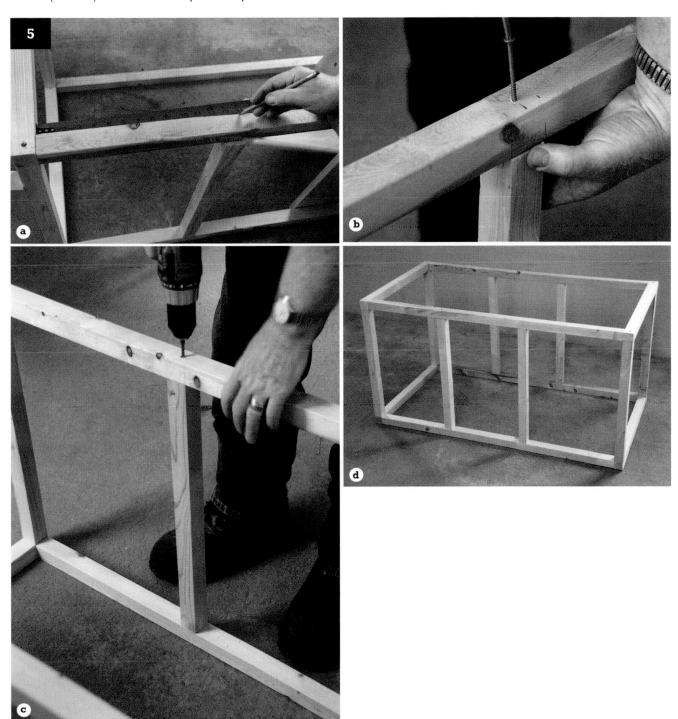

STEP-BY-STEP

6 BUILD A SHADE AREA. Now the ten 25 in. (63.5 cm) 1×6s come into use to create a shaded area on one end of the rabbit tractor. Using a finish nailer (if you have one—you can also use screws, or hand nail this), fasten four of the 1×6s across the short end of the frame (ideally these should fit exactly, but you might have to tap them in with your hammer if the fit is too tight). Then use an additional three 25 in. (63.5 cm) 1×6s on each long side of the frame as shown. When finished, these side 1×6s should line up exactly with the side brace you centered at 27¾ in. (70.5 cm).

7 FINISH THE ROOF. Now take the roof frame you built in step 4 and nail the five 4 ft. (122 cm) 1×6s across the top to create a solid roof. You'll notice that the last 1×6 is too wide and extends off the edge of the frame; this is used as the handle for raising and lowering the roof; the hinges will mount on the opposite side. Use the finish nailer to fasten the 1×6s, but be sure to add a layer of wood glue to this joint for additional strength.

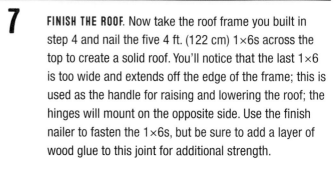

8 **CUT THE HARDWARE CLOTH.** Using wire snips or tin snips, carefully measure and cut out your hardware cloth sections. You'll definitely want to wear proper gloves and eye protection while doing this. For the two open areas on the long sides of the rabbit tractor, cut out two 30 × 24½ in. (76.2 × 62.2 cm) sections. For the single open short end, cut a 2 × 2 ft. (61 × 61 cm) square.

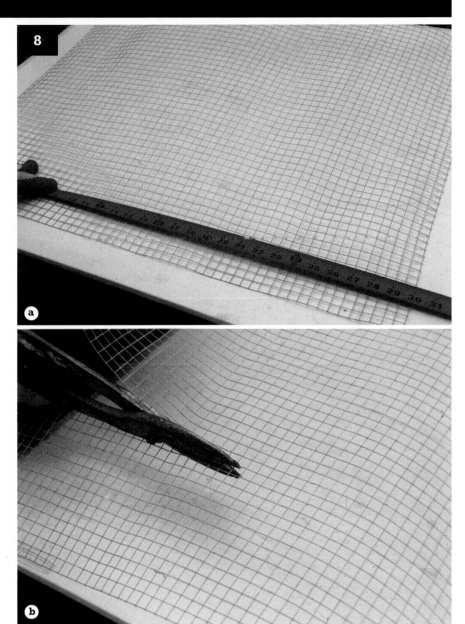

STEP-BY-STEP

9 **FASTEN THE HARDWARE CLOTH.** There are a few ways you can fasten the hardware cloth to the rabbit tractor; we used a staple gun for speed and ease, although you may have to keep a hammer on hand to tap down staples that don't fully set on their own. Alternatively, you could use a hammer and short roofing nails to pin down the hardware cloth. In general, while working with the hardware cloth, it helps to have a second person to aid you.

9

10 ADD HINGES TO THE ROOF. Now you can attach the roof to the main rabbit tractor frame. We set our 2 in. (51 mm) hinges in about 6 in. (152 mm) from each end. You can also add a hook and eye latch for a bit more security.

11 ADD HANDLES. A rabbit tractor should ideally be simple to move around, so adding a set of handles on each end will help make this task easier. We just took two final 25 in. (63.5 cm) 2×2s and screwed them onto the short ends of the rabbit tractor, up near the top of the main frame (not on the roof). This simple addition gives you a convenient place to lift the rabbit tractor. Now place your rabbit tractor in a good location, and let your rabbits enjoy it!

Make Cottage Cheese

SKILL LEVEL:
Easy

TIME REQUIRED:
1 to 2 hours

When dairy cows or dairy goats are present on a farm, the emphasis, naturally, tends to be on milk production. It might be fresh milk just for the family, or it might be part of a larger farm production that provides milk for sale; either way, the twice-daily task of milking tends to focus primarily on just that: milk. This is fine, but there are other areas of dairy production that shouldn't be overlooked, and those are wonderful things like cheeses, yogurts, and even cottage cheese.

TOOLS NEEDED

- Large stock pot
- Spoon
- Strainer or cheesecloth
- Large bowl
- Candy thermometer or digital thermometer

INGREDIENTS

- 1 gallon (3.78 L) of pasteurized milk
- 1 cup (240 mL) of vinegar
- Salt to taste

The processes behind making these products are interesting and perhaps a little challenging—the perfect combination for the experienced farm DIYer. Plus, it opens up an entire new world of possibilities for using the milk from your dairy animals. Cheeses, yogurts, and cottage cheese can also stay fresh at least a little longer than fresh milk—extending the storage of your "harvest" in a similar (though not as long term) way as canning or freezing can do for fruits and vegetables from your garden.

For this project, we thought we'd take a closer look at the process involved with making cottage cheese,

since it's a dairy product you can make in your own kitchen fairly easily. It doesn't take an extraordinarily long time to prepare and creates a very tasty final product. But there are other benefits, too—cottage cheese is a very good source of protein, as well as calcium and some of the B vitamins. As with weaving with wool from your own sheep or making applesauce from your own apples, preparing cottage cheese like this from your own animals' milk is a fun way to make something real and meaningful from your own efforts—and that is a great accomplishment.

STEP-BY-STEP

1 **HEAT THE MILK.** In the large stock pot, heat the milk to 180° Fahrenheit (82° Celcius). Use your candy thermometer or digital thermometer to be sure you've reached the right temperature. Stir the milk every once in a while to make sure it's not sticking to the bottom of the pot.

157

STEP-BY-STEP

2 **ADD VINEGAR.** When your milk is just barely beginning to boil (you should see bubbles starting to rise), take it off the heat. Add the vinegar and stir until curds begin to form. This should happen fairly quickly. You can also add the salt at this step, or wait until the end.

3 **LET COOL.** Once you see curds beginning to form, stop stirring the milk, and let it cool. You can test for firmness with your fingers.

4 **SEPARATE THE CURDS.** When your curds are cool, separate them from the whey. You can use a strainer or cheesecloth. You'll end up with the curds in the strainer and the whey in a bowl. Discard the whey.

5 **RINSE THE CURDS**. Rinse your curds under cold water to remove any remaining whey. Whey can make your cottage cheese bitter, so be sure to rinse well!

6 **ADD SALT TO TASTE**. If you haven't added your salt already, now is the time. Enjoy!

Build a Barn Quilt

SKILL LEVEL: Advanced

TIME REQUIRED:
Several days (including
drying time between
coats of paint)

Think your beautifully repainted barn needs a little something extra to spruce it up? Maybe it looks a little plain from the road? Try adding a barn quilt! These delightful wooden decorations are colorful, eye-catching, and enjoyable for both the barn owner and people who might see the quilt while traveling down your road.

CUT LIST

- 2   4 × 8 ft. (122 × 244 cm) MDO (medium density overlay) plywood sheets
- 2   8 ft. (244 cm) treated 2×4s (sides of back frame)
- 3   89 in. (226 cm) treated 2×4s (top, bottom, and center of back frame)
- 6   42¾ in. (106 cm) treated 2×4s (six braces for back frame)
- 4   8 ft. (244 cm) nontreated 2×4s (for front trim)

PARTS LIST

- Box of   6 in. (152 mm) exterior screws
- Box of   1½ in. (38 mm) exterior screws
- Box of   3 in. (76 mm) exterior screws
- 1 gallon (3.78 L) latex exterior primer
- 1 gallon (3.78 L) latex exterior white low-sheen paint
- 1 gallon (3.78 L) latex exterior red low-sheen paint

Note: Additional screws/fasteners will be required to hang the quilt; the exact types and lengths will depend on your building and situation.

TOOLS NEEDED

- Circular saw/miter saw (a miter saw can be helpful in making the miter cuts on the trim, but isn't required)
- Electric drill
- Wood glue
- Tape measure
- Pencil
- Framing square
- Triangle square
- Level (a long level is helpful here)
- Caulking gun
- Wood clamps
- Paintbrushes
- Paint rollers
- Painting tape
- Utility knife
- Paint scraper
- Construction adhesive (optional)

The patterns on barn quilts are usually taken from old quilt block designs. The modern barn quilt "movement" seems to have originated in Ohio and has rapidly spread throughout rural America; some locations with many barn quilts even promote barn quilt "tours" where tourists can follow a map to drive by many different barn quilts in a day.

Don't be daunted by the size of the barn quilt described in this project. We made an 8 × 8 ft. (244 × 244 cm) barn quilt to fill the space on our 40 ft. (12m)-wide barn, but you can easily downsize the project to 6 × 6 ft. (183 × 183 cm), 4 × 4 ft. (122 × 122 cm), or even 2 × 2 (61 × 61 cm) to hang on a shed, garage, or even inside your house. The instructions included here are for an 8 × 8 ft. (244 × 244 cm) barn quilt painted on MDO ("sign") plywood and mounted to a wooden frame, which is in turn mounted on the side of a barn or other large building. When you're finished, you'll have added a charming bit of folk art to your property.

STEP-BY-STEP

1 **PREPARE THE LUMBER.** The only way to begin a big project like this is to just jump in and start. Begin by preparing the various lengths of 2×4s. Remember, even if you purchase 8 ft. (244 cm) 2×4s, they will most likely be a bit longer than this and will need to be trimmed down to exactly 96 in. (244 cm). Now is also a fine time to make the 45° miter cuts on the four untreated 2×4s; these will eventually become the trim for the barn quilt. For the face of the barn quilt, we used exterior grade MDO (medium density overlay) plywood, which is a type of plywood sandwiched between two smooth outer layers that make an excellent surface for signs and will work perfectly for the barn quilt.

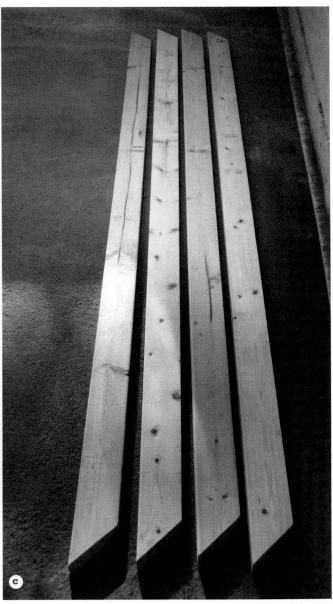

2

ASSEMBLE THE BACK FRAME PERIMETER. Now let the construction begin. Take the two treated 8 ft. (244 cm) 2×4s and use them as sides for a large 8 ft. (244 cm) square; take two of the 89 in. (226 cm) 2×4s and use them as the top and bottom. This will form the barn quilt's exact 8 × 8 ft. (244 × 244 cm) footprint. To make the construction process easier, we used four sawhorses, one to support each corner of the quilt frame. Use a framing square to help achieve square corners, and then fasten with wood glue and 6 in. (152 mm) exterior screws. Throughout the framing process, you might find it helpful to prepare all of the screws by getting them started first, and only drive them in fully once everything is in place.

Note: This back frame is for supporting the back of the barn quilt and will be covered by the MDO plywood. Also, in the photo series, the top of the photo is the top of the barn quilt.

STEP-BY-STEP

3 **CHECK FOR SQUARENESS.** On a project of this size, achieving a square frame might require more than just checking each corner with the framing square. So at this point it's a good idea to measure *diagonally* from corner to corner both ways across the frame and see how close the two diagonal measurements are. If they don't match and are slightly off, you'll want to gently push or pull on different corners to adjust the squareness until the two measurements match.

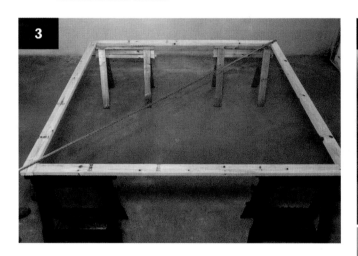

4 **ADD THE CENTER SUPPORT.** Now you can add a center support to the frame; this is where the seam of the two 4 × 8 ft. (122 × 244 cm) sheets of MDO plywood will meet. Use the last 89 in. (226 cm) 2×4 for the center support positioned between the 89 in. (226 cm) top and bottom 2×4s. The center support should be centered right at 4 ft. (122 cm). As with all of the framing construction steps, fasten with wood glue and 6 in. (152 mm) exterior screws.

5 **INSTALL ADDITIONAL BRACES.** Six 42¾ in. (106 cm) 2×4s are used as additional braces on the frame, all with the purpose of tightly securing the MDO plywood so it won't warp or buckle. Each of them fit between one of the frame's sides and the center support, and each should be centered at 2, 4, and 6 ft. (61, 122, and 244 cm) respectively, as shown. At this point, you should have the completed back frame for the barn quilt, made entirely of treated 2×4s.

6 **ADD PRIMER TO THE PLYWOOD.**
Now we set the frame aside for a little while and get to work on the actual barn quilt itself. During these first phases of the priming, painting, and planning stages, it might be easier to keep the two 4 × 8 ft. (122 × 244 cm) sheets of plywood on separate sets of sawhorses, as we did here. Using your exterior primer, paint the edges of the plywood first, taking care to work the primer well into the rough edges so that rainwater won't penetrate later on and shorten the life of the barn quilt. A roller can be used on the main surface to speed up the work. We used two coats of primer on both sides of each piece, allowing it to dry between coats.

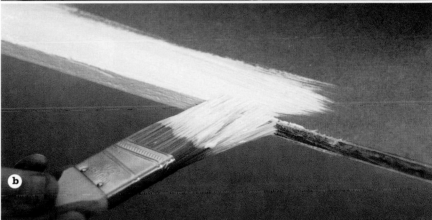

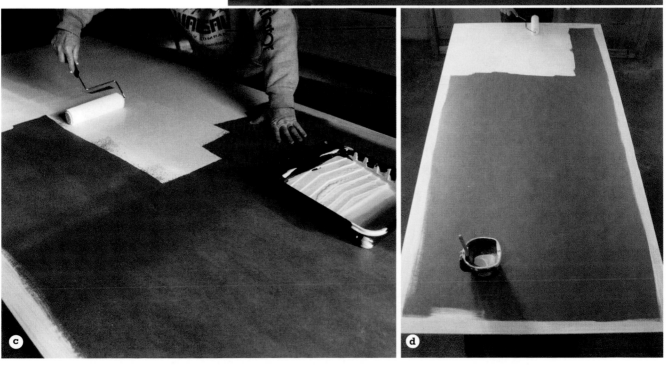

STEP-BY-STEP

7 ADD **PRIMER TO THE TRIM**. While you're waiting for the primer to dry on the main barn quilt, now is a good time to also put the primer coats on the barn quilt's trim—the four 8 ft. (244 cm) 2×4s with mitered edges.

8 ADD **WHITE PAINT**. Once the coats of primer have dried, you can begin painting the MDO plywood with your exterior white paint. Again, make sure to paint the edges well. We used two coats of white.

9 PAINT **THE TRIM**. While the white paint on the MDO dries, you can apply the first coat of red paint on the four 8 ft. (244 cm) trim pieces. Once they have dried, add a second coat to ensure the best look. Set these aside for installation later on.

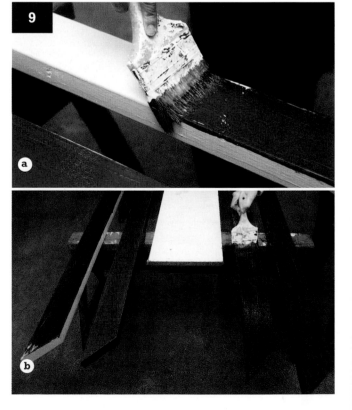

10 ADD PENCIL LINES FOR THE DESIGN. Painter's tape is needed to mask off the edges of what will become the red areas of the barn quilt. But before putting down tape, it's helpful to lay out the complete barn quilt design in pencil. You can put both MDO sheets side by side to help you visualize the complete quilt, or you can keep them separate to make it easier to reach the center areas; do whatever works best for you. Using a level as a straightedge (a longer level is helpful for this), first mark off a 3½ in. (89 mm) border around the whole perimeter of the barn quilt. Next, pencil off an 8 × 8 grid pattern, with each square 11⅛ in. (282 mm) long on each side (the squares would all be 12 in. [305 mm] if not for the space taken up by the perimeter trim). Finally, use our final project photos as a guide to marking off the rest of the design (or whatever design you've chosen). A framing square can help with this part quite a bit. We also added the letter "R" for Red on each section that should be painted in that color. Note that for the pattern we used, each square in the grid is either all white, all red, or diagonally half red/white.

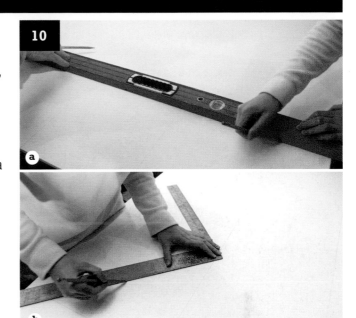

11 ATTACH THE PLYWOOD TO THE FRAME. At this stage we attached the two MDO sheets to the frame we built. In order to avoid placing screws on the visible face of the barn quilt, we used construction adhesive for the center areas, but then fastened the edges (which will be underneath the 2×4 trim boards) with 1½ in. (38 mm) exterior screws. You could also choose to fasten the face of the quilt with screws, and then cover the visible heads with touch-up paint. Also, the joint between the two MDO sheets may need to be caulked, if there is a visible gap.

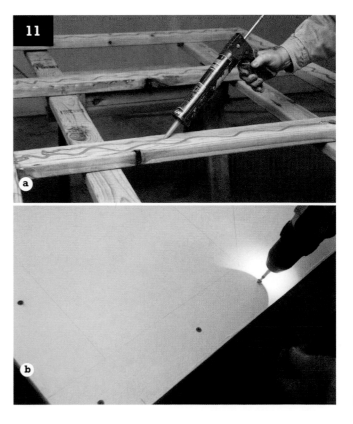

STEP-BY-STEP

12 MASK OFF THE EDGES. Now use painter's tape to mask off all the edges between the future white and red areas, using your pencil marks as guides. (You may need to set the barn quilt up vertically for this step and the next one.) After this step, you can start to see what the barn quilt will look like when finished!

13 PAINT THE PATTERN. At last! Grab your red paint and actually begin painting in the barn quilt's pattern. This step should be fairly simple, really—just make sure you don't paint over the tape and into the white areas. Just as a reminder for ourselves as we worked, we marked the all-white squares with a dot of green painter's tape. Once dried, apply a second—or perhaps even a third—coat.

14 REMOVE THE PAINTER'S TAPE. With the pattern fully finished, it's time to remove the painter's tape and admire the finished design! You might also take this moment to touch-up any red paint that seeped under the tape.

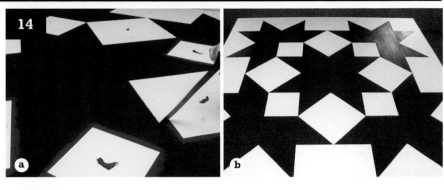

15 ADD TRIM. Now you can take your four pieces of red trim and screw them to the edges of the barn quilt with 3 in. (76 mm) screws. To make sure that the miter joints fit together tightly, you might need to scrape any excess dried paint off the mitered edges. You can also use your construction adhesive here, or use wood glue as we did. Wood clamps can help hold the trim in place while you screw from underneath—screwing from below prevents screw holes on the face of the trim.

16 PAINT THE EDGES. The edges of the barn quilt's frame—while protected by the pressure treating process—will look better if two coats of red paint are added. The only remaining step now is to actually install it on the side of your barn; the exact process here will depend on your barn's height, construction, siding type, etc. For tall structures, it may well be worth the expense to hire a professional to install it for you.

Graft a Fruit Tree

SKILL LEVEL:
Easy

TIME REQUIRED:
1 hour

Planting an apple tree or other fruit tree is easy, right? Isn't it just like Johnny Appleseed, where you just toss a few tree seeds in the ground and they grow into your favorite varieties? Well, not quite. While it's theoretically true that you could plant a seed from your favorite apple tree—say a Wolf River apple tree—and it could grow into a new tree, the problem is that the new tree won't share the exact genetics of its Wolf River parent. The new tree will be a *hybrid* of a Wolf River and some other random apple tree from the area—whatever it was cross-pollinated with. You might occasionally glean a useful and tasty apple from a tree pollinated in this manner, but in general the results will likely be disappointing. So, what's the alternative?

TOOLS NEEDED

- Tape measure
- Pruning loppers
- Sharp knife
- Chisel
- Hammer
- Grafting wax or asphalt-water emulsion

Note: There are many specialized grafting tools available, including grafting knives and chisels, but unless you're grafting a lot of trees, care and patience will allow you to make do with more general tools.

The answer lies in *grafting*, and we'll look at one simple type of graft in this project. When you graft a fruit tree, you're essentially performing a low-tech cloning process, taking the genetics of one donor tree and propagating them on a new host rootstock or branch. The graft branch (with the original desirable genetics, called the *scion*) will take nutrients and water from the new host tree or rootstock, but will produce apples that are exact clones of ones from the original tree. This is how popular apple varieties have been preserved for decades and even centuries. McIntosh, Red Delicious, Granny Smith—all these

varieties and more owe their current existence and perennial popularity to the science—or may we say art?—of grafting.

Successful grafting is challenging indeed, but we'll look at one simple type of graft here: the cleft graft. The tools required are minimal and it doesn't take much time, so why not give it a try? You might be able to join in the tradition of preserving an apple variety you enjoy. It can also be a good way to finally get better fruit from a poorly producing tree, like a crab apple.

STEP-BY-STEP

1   **CHOOSE YOUR SCIONS.** The best scion wood is young and vigorous—preferably, it will come from a branch that grew substantially within the last year, adding at least a foot (30.5 cm) to its length. In many cases this is readily noticeable; there will be a point along the branch where it subtly changes color, indicating where the youngest growth began. You don't need to worry about the diameter of the branch, since young growth is by definition not very thick.

Once you've found an ideal branch, cut off a section at least 4 in. (101 mm) long, if not a bit longer. Just as important to consider is the number of buds on each 4 in. (101 mm) piece; three is a good number to aim for. Aim to have a good bud located about 2 in. (51 mm) above the cut end of the scion. A long piece of ideal scion wood can be subdivided into multiple pieces.

If you intend to cut your scion wood and perform the grafting at different times, the scions should be wrapped in a damp towel (paper towels work fine) and refrigerated.

STEP-BY-STEP

2 **PREPARE THE END OF THE SCION.**
In order to be installed in a cleft graft, the base of the scion must first be prepared. Make slanted cuts on opposite sides, tapering to a blunt point (ideally not a fine point). This can be accomplished by slowly and carefully slicing away wood using your knife. Aim to make the slanted cuts about 1½ in. (38 mm) long, with a bud just above the ends of the cuts, and oriented so that the bud is located on an undisturbed side of the branch. Thus, the tapered point should run parallel with the bud, with the point on the bud's side of the branch being slightly wider than the point on the opposite side.

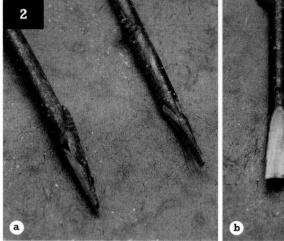
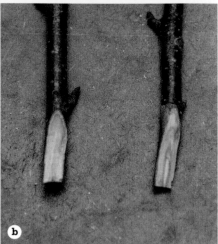

3 **PREPARE THE STOCK WOOD.** For a cleft graft to have the best chance at succeeding, the stock wood should be at least ¾ in. (19 mm) thick, but no thicker than 2 in. (51 mm). Use your pruning loppers to make a flat cut in the branch, but take care to make the cut in an ideal location along the branch. It won't do you any good to cut off the stock close to the tree trunk, or where the stock branches off from a larger limb. Give yourself some wiggle room and cut the stock 12 in. (305 mm) away from any such junctures, though a few inches (or centimeters) less is acceptable.

Once you have made the cut, use a chisel and hammer to split the stock down the middle, opening a crevice at least 2 in. (51 mm) deep.

4   **INSERT THE SCION WOOD.** Take one or two scions and insert them into the crevice in the stock wood, with their buds facing outward. Just underneath the bark lies the green cambium layer that is the living, growing portion of the wood. The key is to ensure that the cambium of the scion wood is properly aligned with the cambium of the stock wood. Don't worry about lining up the bark to make it look even—that's unimportant. Just make sure that those thin cambium layers are in contact with each other.

5   **SEAL THE GRAFT.** Follow the instructions for using your waxing graft or asphalt-water emulsion and seal the graft completely, covering all cracks and exposed areas to protect the wood from drying out. Once the cuts are sealed, you should be good to go! Now you just have to wait until spring to see if your graft was successful. If you installed two pieces of scion wood and both survive, favor the more vigorous one during future prunings; eventually, the weaker half can be pruned off completely.

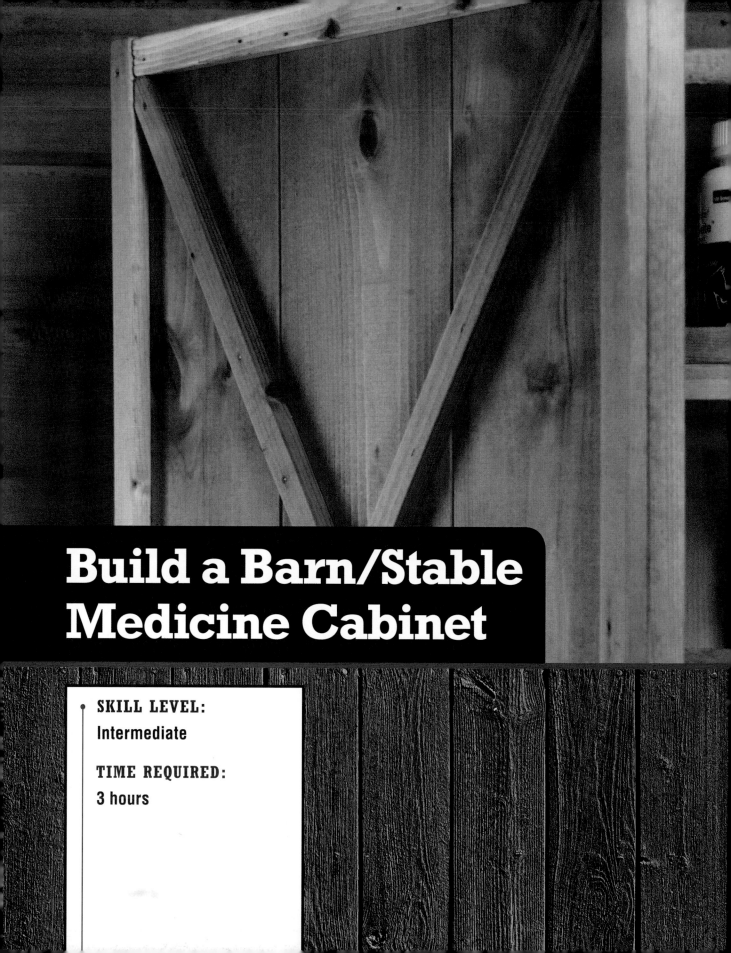

Build a Barn/Stable Medicine Cabinet

SKILL LEVEL:
Intermediate

TIME REQUIRED:
3 hours

When you have livestock, it's always wise to be prepared ahead of time and have supplies on hand to treat the occasional injury or illness. You also probably have various supplements and other preventive medicines that need to be kept handy. No matter what kind of livestock you raise—sheep, goats, horses, cattle—stocking and maintaining an assortment of ointments, wound-cleaning supplies, and bandages puts you one step ahead if something does go wrong.

CUT LIST

FOR THE CABINET

• 6	22 in. (55.9 cm)	1×6s (back wall and door)
• 2	20½ in. (52.1 cm)	1×6s (two sides)
• 2	16½ in. (41.9 cm)	1×6s (top and bottom)
• 2	15 in. (38.1 cm)	1×6s (two shelves)
• 1	5½ in. (140 mm)	1×6 (shelf divider)

FOR THE TRIM

• 2	22 in. (55.9 cm)	½ × ¾ in. (13 × 19 mm) trim (sides of door)
• 4	15 in. (38.1 cm)	½ × ¾ in. (13 × 19 mm) trim (top and bottom of door, plus two shelf edges)
• 2	25½ in. (64.8 cm)	½ × ¾ in. (13 × 19 mm) trim (diagonal pieces of door)
• 2	7⅛ in. (181 mm)	½ × ¾ in. (13 × 19 mm) trim (shelf edges for small shelves)

PARTS LIST

- 2   2 in. (51 mm) hinges
- Box of 1½ in. (38 mm) finish nails
- Box of 1 in. (25 mm) finish nails
- Box of 1½ in. (38 mm) screws (for fastening to wall)

With that in mind, here's our next project: a basic medicine cabinet that will hold some of your livestock medical supplies in a nice-looking cabinet that will be an attractive addition to your barn or stable. You may not need to access these items daily, but it's important to have them in a central location where everyone on the farm knows where to find them—and there's no reason why the cabinet shouldn't look nice, too. This design features a swinging door, two larger shelves, and two smaller shelves to hold a variety of items of different sizes. The door of the cabinet is designed to be reminiscent of a barn or stable door, which helps it fit in well with a barn or stable setting.

TOOLS NEEDED

- Circular saw
- Jigsaw
- Finish nailer (or hammer and electric drill for pre-drilling holes)
- Framing square
- Triangle square
- Level
- Tape measure
- Pencil
- Sandpaper
- Screwdriver (for attaching hinges)
- Wood glue
- Wood clamps

STEP-BY-STEP

1 **MAKE CUTS.** The medicine cabinet is made entirely out of 1×6 materials, except for the door and shelf trim, so start out by making all of the required cuts of the 1×6s. A circular saw or miter saw will make quick work of this job. The trim pieces we used were all ½ × ¾ in. (13 × 19 mm), which should be ripped from larger material using a table saw.

2 **SAND THE EDGES.** To make a nicer final product, go ahead and sand all the edges of the 1×6s at this point to remove any rough points.

STEP-BY-STEP

3 ASSEMBLE THE BASIC FRAME. It's a simple matter to construct the basic overall frame of the medicine cabinet. Use the two 20½ in. (52.1 cm) 1×6s as sides and the two 16½ in. (41.9 cm) 1×6s as the top and bottom, making sure that the 20½ in. (52.1 cm) sides go "inside" the 16½ in. (41.9 cm) top and bottom, as shown. It can be helpful to use a framing square to get the corners exactly 90°. Use 1½ in. (38 mm) nails to fasten.

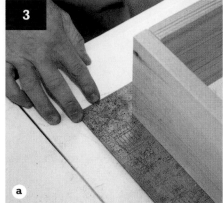

a

b

4 ADD THE BACK WALL. Now take three of the 22 in. (55.9 cm) 1×6s and use them to form the back wall of the medicine cabinet; they should fit over the basic frame exactly. Again, use 1½ in. (38 mm) nails for assembly.

a

b

c

d

5

ADD THE TOP SHELF. At this stage you can add in the cabinet's shelves. The top horizontal shelf is 15 in. (38.1 cm) long, and is divided in half by the 5½ in. (140 mm) 1×6 divider. A triangle square can be handy here for keeping the shelf straight while you nail it into position.

6

ADD THE SECOND SHELF. The second 15 in. (38.1 cm) horizontal shelf should be separated from the top shelf by about 5½ in. (140 mm). This creates one lower area that is larger than the upper two shelves, handy for storing taller items in the cabinet.

STEP-BY-STEP

7 **CONSTRUCT THE DOOR.** The door is made from three 22 in. (55.9 cm) 1×6s, fastened together with the door's trim pieces. To start, use a finish nailer and 1 in. (25 mm) nails to create a border around the three 22 in. (55.9 cm) 1×6s using 22 In. (55.9 cm) trim on the sides and 15 in. (38.1 cm) for the top and bottom. The top and bottom trim fit "inside" the longer pieces as shown.

8

INSTALL THE FIRST DIAGONAL TRIM. Now take one of the 25½ in. (64.8 cm) trim pieces and position it diagonally across the door as shown. Using a pencil (a ruler might help, too) carefully mark lines on the corners where a jigsaw can be used to make the corner cuts. After cutting with the jigsaw, use sandpaper to smooth out the edges.

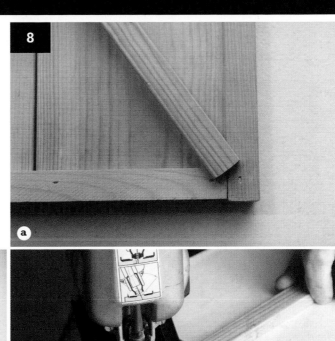

a

b

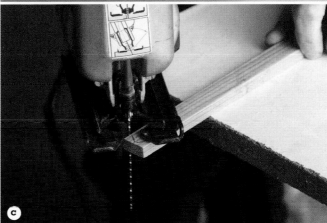

c

d

e

STEP-BY-STEP

9 **INSTALL THE OTHER DIAGONAL TRIM.**
The second 25½ in. (64.8 cm)
trim piece goes diagonally across
the door in the other direction,
and requires similar corner cuts
on each end like the first one.
You'll also need to mark and make
two cuts in the center of this
piece—creating two shorter trim
pieces that will fit between the
first one as shown. Use a finish
nailer to fasten all the trim.

a

b

c

10 **ADD SHELF EDGES.** Next use wood glue to attach additional pieces of trim to the edges of the interior shelves. The goal here is to prevent bottles and small items from rolling off the shelves. Two 15 in. (38.1 cm) trim pieces are used for the wide shelves, and two 7⅛ in. (181 mm) pieces are used for the two shorter upper shelves. Use wood clamps to hold them in place until the glue dries.

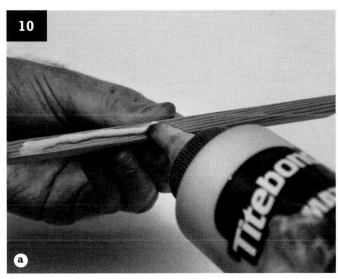

(a)

(b)

11 **STAIN.** If you'd like, give your medicine cabinet a more finished look by adding a coat or two of wood stain in a shade you like. Now is a good time to do this, before the hinges are added.

STEP-BY-STEP

12 **ATTACH THE HINGES.** We used two 2 in. (51 mm) hinges to attach the door to the cabinet, with each hinge set in 2 in. (51 mm). Pre-drilling the holes can make it easier to attach them.

13   **HANG THE CABINET.** With the stain dry and the door attached, the cabinet is now ready to hang on the wall! Use a level to get it straight, and then use 1½ in. (38 mm) screws to attach the back of the cabinet onto a wooden wall. Fill it up with the livestock medical supplies that you find most handy to have around.

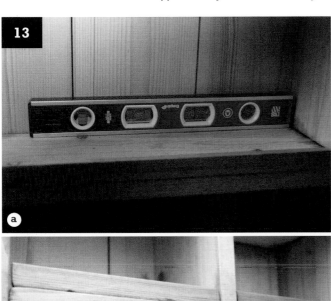

INDEX

ABOUT THE AUTHORS

Brother-and-sister collaborators **Samantha Johnson** and **Daniel Johnson** pursue their writing, photography, and agricultural interests at the family-owned Fox Hill and Pine Valley Farms in northern Wisconsin. Since 1999, they have raised and shown registered Welsh Mountain ponies, and they also enjoy the company of the several hundred thousand honey bees at Fox Hill and Pine Valley.

Samantha is an award-winning writer, as well as a proofreader and pony wrangler. She is a certified show judge with the Wisconsin State Horse Council and the Welsh Pony and Cob Society of America. She has written multiple books, including several on rabbits and a beginning vegetable-gardening guide (coauthored with Daniel). Samantha also enjoys fulfilling the demands of her bossy Corgi, Peaches.

Writer and photographer Daniel likes to spend his time lugging around heavy camera equipment in all kinds of weather to take pictures of everything from dogsledding in freezing temperatures to hay-baling in the heat of summer. He loves to photograph horses as well and is the coauthor (with Samantha) and photographer of several horse books. In his spare time, he also photographs frogs, one of which has been his pet for more than twenty-five years.